HUMAN RIGHTS
IN
AFRICA

HUMAN RIGHTS IN AFRICA

A Comparative Study of the African Human and People's Rights Charter and the New Tanzanian Bill of Rights

Chris Maina Peter

Published under the auspices of the Consortium on Human Rights Development

Studies in Human Rights, Number 10
George W. Shepherd, Jr., Series Editor

Greenwood Press
New York • Westport, Connecticut • London

Library of Congress Cataloging-in-Publication Data

Peter, Chris Maina, 1954-
  Human rights in Africa.

  (Studies in human rights, ISSN 0146-3586 ; no. 10)
  Includes bibliographical references.
  1. Civil rights—Tanzania. 2. Human rights—Africa.
I. Title. II. Series.
LAW   342.678'085   89-17126
           346.780285
ISBN 0-313-26863-0 (lib. bdg. : alk. paper)

British Library Cataloguing in Publication Data is available.

Library of Congress Catalog Card Number: 89-17126
ISBN: 0-313-26863-0
ISSN: 0146-3586

First published in 1990

Greenwood Press, Inc.
88 Post Road West, Westport, Connecticut 06881

Printed in the United States of America

The paper used in this book complies with the
Permanent Paper Standard issued by the National
Information Standards Organization (Z39.48-1984).

10 9 8 7 6 5 4 3 2 1

To Brigitte Veronika Klemm
for her unwavering feminist militancy

Contents

Abbreviations

AMNUT	All Muslim National Union of Tanganyika
ASP	Afro-Shirazi Party
CCM	Chama Cha Mapinduzi
CRDI	Congolese Industrial Waste Recovery Company
Doc.	Document
ECA	United Nations Economic Commission for Africa
ECOWAS	Economic Community of West African States
EEC	European Economic Community
EEE	European Entente for the Environment
EPA	Environmental Protection Agency (US)
FFU	Field Force Unit
GDR	German Democratic Republic
G.N.	Government Notice
IAEA	International Atomic Energy Agency
ICJ	International Court of Justice
IMF	International Monetary Fund
infra	below
JUWATA	Jumuiya ya Wafanyakazi wa Tanzania
KCC	Kima Cha Chini
MBLD	Beninois pour la Liberte et la Democratie
Mimeo.	mimeograph
Mv.	marine vehicle
NEC	National Executive Committee
NIEO	New International Economic Order
No.	number
NPF	National Provident Fund
NUTA	National Union of Tanzanian Workers
OAU	Organization of African Unity
PTA	Preferential Trade Area
R.	Republic or Rex
SADCC	Southern African Development Co-ordination Conference
SHIHATA	Shirika la Habari Tanzania
supra	above
TANU	Tanganyika African National Union
TFL	Tanganyika Federation of Labour
Tshs.	Tanzanian shillings
UN	United Nations
UNCTAD	United Nations Conference on Trade and Development
UWT	United Women of Tanzania
UNEP	United Nations Environment Program
UNO	United Nations Organization
US$	United States dollar

Acknowledgments

In the process of preparing this work, a lot of people assisted us in various ways. It is not possible to mention all of them here. However, we would like to note the special assistance we received from the following friends and colleagues and wholeheartedly thank them.

First, Bagi Oesterreich, who initiated the whole idea of comparing the Tanzanian Bill of Rights and the African Charter on Human and People's Rights; second, my friend and colleague Rainer Michael Bierwagen, who tirelessly read the many drafts of the work and made valuable comments; third, Emmanuel De Dios of the University of the Philippines, who was on sabbatical leave at the University of Konstanz in the academic year 1987/88, for reading the draft of the work and taking keen interest in it; fourth, Rose Mtengeti-Migiro for reading part of the draft and pointing out errors; George Kahabuka, through whom we were able to get papers on Tanzania which kept us up-to-date on the events at home; and Gitte for support during the preparation of the work.

Last, but not least, we would like to thank Professor Carsten-Thomas Ebenroth of the Faculty of Law, University of Konstanz, for putting his massive secretarial facilities at our disposal. Without his assistance, this work would have taken years to complete.

Chapter 1
The Tanzanian Bill of Rights
and the African Charter
on Human and People's Rights:
An Historical Background

> This document (the African Charter on Human and
> People's Rights) should be like a lady's skirt. Long
> enough to cover the subject matter; but short enough
> to be interesting.
>
> T. O. Elias(1)

This study is a modest attempt to examine the newly enacted
Bill of Rights in the recent amendment to the Constitution
of the United Republic of Tanzania(2) in light of the
provisions of the Organization of African Unity's African
Charter on Human and People's Rights.(3) Both documents
center on what are known as basic or fundamental rights of
the individual, whose importance must be clear to all.
    The difference between these two documents is twofold.
First, while the Tanzanian Bill of Rights is a national
law, specifically applying only in one country, the
African Charter is a regional instrument applying to
countries signatory to it. The latter is therefore general
and has a wider application. Second, the African Charter
came into force on October 21, 1986,(4) two years before
the Tanzanian Bill of Rights, which became effective on
March 15, 1988.(5) Another feature worth noting is that
while the Tanzanian Bill of Rights restricts itself to the
basic rights, freedoms, and duties of the individual, the
African Charter goes further by including what are termed
people's rights. These are rights an individual can enjoy
only in a collective sense as a member of a community.(6)
This is an essential development in conceptualization of
human rights in general.

BILL OF RIGHTS IN TANZANIA

As the colonies were nearing independence in the 1950s and
1960s, the issue of a Bill of Rights abruptly rose in
importance on every agenda. It was given a special place,
particularly in negotiations for independence between the
colonial powers and the nationalists. The British, who
once boasted that the sun never set on their empire, are
famous for insisting that each of their colonies moving to

independence should entrench a Bill of Rights in its constitution. By 1973 about 32 of the former British colonies had a Bill of Rights in their constitutions.(7) Tanzania (then Tanganyika) was an exception.(8)

However, the British insistence on Bills of Rights in their former colonies should not be interpreted as a purely humanitarian gesture toward the indigenous peoples. One main worry of the British government was the security of the British citizens and subjects resident in the colonies and their property. These heavy investments in the colonies could not be phased out immediately after the political power had changed hands and required protection and constitutional safeguards. This partly explains the sudden and belated concern on the part of the colonial rulers over democracy, the rule of law, and Bills of Rights in the newly independent states.

The nationalists in Tanganyika led by the Tanganyika African National Union (TANU) raised two main arguments against the inclusion of a Bill of Rights in the independence constitution. First, Tanganyika was a young nation, faced with tremendous problems of nation-building and economic development. It therefore required a constitutional form appropriate for an independent African state and capable of inspiring a sense of loyalty in the people of Tanganyika. In such a constitutional form, a Bill of Rights was deemed inappropriate as it would have hindered the new government in executing its developmental plans for the people.(9) Second, the judiciary in the country was still staffed by expatriates--mainly whites engaged by the former colonial government. These judicial officers could have taken advantage of the presence of a Bill of Rights in the constitution to frustrate the new government by declaring many of its actions illegal. In the words of then Prime Minister Rashid Kawawa, "a Bill of Rights merely invites conflicts of luxury which we could hardly afford to entertain."(10) The Bill of Rights was therefore shelved.(11)

The issue of the Bill of Rights surfaced again in the country-wide debate on the proposals by the National Executive Committee (NEC) of TANU on the establishment of a democratic one-party state. The president had been instructed by the party to establish a commission on one-party democracy.(12) The terms of reference of this commission were clearly explained by the president. It was not supposed to deliberate on whether Tanganyika should be a one-party state or not. That had already been decided by the party. The commission was simply supposed to deliberate and invite comments and ideas from the public on the implementation of the party decision. In the president's own words:

> In order to avoid misunderstanding, I think I
> should emphasize that it is not the task of the
> Commission to consider whether Tanganyika should be a
> One-Party State. The decision has already been taken.
> Their task is to say what kind of One-Party State we
> should have in the context of our national ethic and
> in accordance with the principles I have instructed
> the Commission to observe.(13)

The Tanganyika Law Society, which is a society of practicing advocates and other lawyers in the country, wrote a memorandum to the commission suggesting inter alia that a Bill of Rights be included in the constitution. According to the society, the incorporation of a Bill of Rights which guaranteed the basic rights and freedoms of the individual would ensure universal respect for the constitution.

The well-considered suggestion by the lawyers was conveniently ignored by the government, which instead adopted two other methods of protection of fundamental rights and freedoms. The first method was to provide for fundamental rights and freedoms in a loose and general form in the preamble to the Interim Constitution of 1965.(14) This was not a blind move, and the government might have been well-advised. The preamble is legally not part of the constitution under the common law system. At best, it is a statement of the beliefs of the framers of the constitution. One cannot base a case on it.

The status of the preamble is explained by Justice of Appeal Kisanga of the Court of Appeal of Tanzania in his separate judgment in <u>Attorney-General vs. Lesinoi Ndenai and Two Others</u>.(15) His Lordship explained that the preamble was "a declaration of our belief in these rights. It is no more than just that. The rights themselves do not become enacted thereby such that they could be enforced under the Constitution. In other words, one cannot bring a complaint under the Constitution in respect of violation of any of these rights as enumerated in the Preamble."

However, there was a way to get around this technicality. The Interim Constitution of 1965 had the party constitution (TANU constitution) appended to it as a schedule. The TANU constitution contained provisions on individual rights and freedoms and other guarantees similar to those in the preamble.(16) The schedule, unlike the preamble, is technically part of the constitution. Therefore, while one could not base a complaint on the preamble, one could successfully protest against violation of rights through the schedule. This was tried successfully in 1973 in the case of <u>Thabit Ngaka vs. Fisheries Officer (Morogoro)</u>.(17) However, all this is history, as things changed with the adoption of the Constitution of the United Republic of Tanzania in 1977.(18) This constitution does not contain the party constitution as a schedule. The second method adopted by the government in dealing with fundamental rights and freedoms was to set up a form of ombudsman (19) known as the Permanent Commission of Enquiry through the Interim Constitution.(20) The idea came from the Presidential Commission on the Establishment of a Democratic One-Party State. The commission had recommended that a Permanent Commission of Enquiry be created, chaired by a high-ranking party official and including two other persons whose duty would be to receive and investigate complaints about party and government administration and report to the president. (21) The powers of the commission and the procedures to be followed in its work were elaborated in the Permanent Commission of Enquiry Act.(22)

The commission, which still exists today, has

jurisdiction to enquire into the conduct of any person in the exercise of his or her office or authority, or in abuse of office.(23)   This covers persons in the service of the United Republic holding office in the party, local government, public corporations, and other institutions.(24) There are two main exceptions. First, the jurisdiction of the commission does not extend to the president of the United Republic of Tanzania or the head of the Executive for Zanzibar.(25)   Second, the commission has no power to question or review judicial decisions of any judge, magistrate, or registrar or any decision of a tribunal established by law for the performance of judicial functions in the exercise of such functions.(26)

The commission can act either on the direction of the president, following a complaint, or suo moto (on its own). To ensure the independence of the commission, its members have been provided with certain constitutional safeguards which include drawing their salaries from the Consolidated Fund.(27) At the same time, the commission is not subject to judicial control.   Hence, none of its proceedings or findings can be challenged, reviewed, quashed, or called into question in any court of law save for lack of jurisdiction.

The practice of the Permanent Commission of Enquiry is not particularly impressive.   It can hardly be said to be a substitute for a Bill of Rights.   Notwithstanding its existence, high-handed bureaucrats still engage in excesses with impunity.   There are, however, a few cases in which the commission has had positive results.   An example is Case No. 1057, discussed at length by Samuel Asante.(28) In this particular case, the complainant, a Tanzanian citizen of Asian origin, alleged that a Regional Commissioner (hereinafter referred to as RC) had suspended his trading license without any justifiable reason.   The commission took up the matter and after investigation, the following factors came to light: one day, the RC concerned, while visiting certain villages, happened to pass near the shop of the complainant.   He saw a little scuffle occurring between children of the complainant and an African.   The scuffle was put to an end and the RC tried to find out the cause of the fight.   The RC alleged that the Asian boys and their mother (the complainant's wife) answered him rudely and that they had no reason to beat the African boy.   Thereupon, he ordered the trading license of the complainant, who was not present at the scene of the scuffle, to be suspended.   The commission, after examining the facts, came to the conclusion that the fight and whatever might have transpired in connection with it had no relevance to the trading license. The case was reported to the president and the license was given back to the owner. This was an extreme case of abuse of power and the commission's timely intervention rescued the victim. However, cases of this nature are rare. The presence of the commission has not substantially assisted in improving the situation as far as abuse of office by bureaucrats in various public institutions is concerned.

The proposals to amend the constitution of the country leading to the 1984 amendments did not come from the people.   They originated in the party.   That being the case

and there having been no consultation, the proposals were
not general but specific. The National Executive Committee
of   the   party specifically pinpointed the areas of the
constitution which   the   party wanted amended: (1) the
powers of the president; (2) consolidation of the authority
of the parliament; (3) strengthening the representative
character of the National Assembly; (4) consolidation of
the union; and (5) consolidation of the people's power.(29)
     It is clear that a Bill of Rights was not contemplated
by the party.   It came later by popular demand. Popular
pressure ultimately proved to be too much for the party to
ignore and a concession had to be made.

BACKGROUND TO THE TANZANIAN BILL OF RIGHTS

     As indicated in the preceding section, after the
suggestion by the Commission on the Establishment of a
Democratic One-Party State that human rights and the rule
of law could be maintained in the country without
necessarily   incorporating   a   Bill of Rights in the
constitution, as far as the party was concerned a Bill of
Rights was no longer an issue.   That is why it never
appeared in the proposals for the amendment of the
constitution.
     However, a large section of the population was not
convinced by the party's position.   The position of this
majority was clearly articulated by two main groups. These
were the academicians (including the practicing lawyers)
and the Zanzibaris.   Individuals everywhere took the
"opportunity" offered by the party to air their views in
very   clear   terms.   They never bothered with the
restrictions set by the National Executive Committee of the
party.   This was done through the radio, newspapers, and
other forms of expression, such as seminars.
     What the masses of the people could not say clearly
was stated for them by the academicians and particularly
the lawyers. The Tanganyika Law Society, whose suggestions
in 1965 were ignored by the One-Party State Commission, was
again in the forefront. It organized a seminar to discuss
the NEC proposals. Various lawyers, from both the academic
field and practice, contributed challenging papers.(30)
The papers and other contributions to this seminar clearly
indicated that the people wanted a change and it would be
fatal to ignore this wish.
     The second pressure group was from Zanzibar. This
group was bold enough to air its views within party organs,
a practice which is not common in Tanzanian politics.
Zanzibaris, unlike their counterparts on the mainland, are
open people who usually say what they like, when and how
they like it. They have a long history of struggles for
democratic rights. This is due to the fact that for a long
time they lived under a very oppressive, feudal system
perpetrated   by   Arabs.   The Arabs practiced racial
discrimination openly with the full support of the British,
who gave the sultan a free hand and chose to be blind to
what was happening on the islands during the colonial
period.
     It is therefore not surprising that in its very first

constitution   after   independence,   Zanzibar,   unlike
Tanganyika, had a Bill of Rights. This was a thoroughgoing
bill   with   eighteen   articles   based   on   the   Universal
Declaration of Human Rights of 1948.(31)

This constitution was, however,   short-lived.   It was
abrogated following the January 12, 1964, revolution.(32)
Chaos and a completely new form of oppression by the state
and its agencies followed.   While claiming to operate
under the rule of law,(33) the government promulgated harsh
decrees ordering, among other things, detention of persons
without trial,(34) confiscation of immovable property,(35)
and restrictions on the rights of individuals to sue for
denial of fundamental rights.(36)   This was followed by
other strange acts and directives by the ruling Revolutionary Council. The most notorious of these was the
"forced marriages" scandal. This involved forcing girls of
Persian origin to marry members of the Revolutionary
Council and other top government functionaries in September 1970.   This led to bitter protests in mainland
Tanzania, Kenya,   and Zanzibar itself.(37)   Following
protests, the government of Zanzibar promised there would
be no more such marriages.   However, the ones already
consummated were left intact.(38)

All these events were completely opposite of what the
Zanzibaris had expected after the revolution which brought
the majority to power after the overthrow of the sultan.
They therefore looked toward union with the mainland as the
only way to break away from this situation.   The death of
the first president of Zanzibar, Abeid Amani Karume, in
1972 and the coming into power of Aboud Jumbe was the
beginning of a new era on the islands. After the merger of
the political parties in the country--TANU on the mainland
and the Afro-Shirazi Party (ASP) in Zanzibar to form Chama
Cha Mapinduzi (CCM)--in 1977, the two parts of the union
were closer, giving the Zanzibaris more forum to air their
views, even against their own government.(39)   It is
believed that it was their articulate argument within the
party that moved the conservative element to accept the
inclusion of a Bill of Rights in the constitution.

This is the way Tanzanians eventually got their basic
rights and freedoms guaranteed under the constitution some
23 years after independence. It was a protracted struggle
with many actors and scenarios, but with a single aim--
namely, assurance that fundamental rights and freedoms
would be respected and protected.

It is interesting to note that during the time of the
debate on the amendment of the constitution in Tanzania,
the question of human rights had already acquired a special
place on the continent due to the adoption of the African
Charter on Human and People's Rights by the Organization
of African Unity (OAU) in Nairobi in 1981. However, this
fact had little, if any, influence on the inclusion of the
Bill of Rights in the constitution. This may be because
the African Charter was not yet in force and therefore not
well-publicized, and also because Tanzanians were more
inward- than outward-looking. They were more worried about
what was happening at home than elsewhere.

HUMAN RIGHTS IN AFRICA

The adoption of the African Charter on Human and People's Rights at the 18th Ordinary Assembly of Heads of State and Government of the Organization of African Unity in Nairobi, Kenya, in June 1981 was an epoch-making event, not only to the over 400 million Africans but to peace-loving and democratic-minded people the world over. It was the crescendo of sporadic and sometimes uncoordinated attempts by different interest groups in Africa to create a legal mechanism that would guarantee fundamental rights and freedoms to the common people.

For many Africans independence had created high expectations, especially regarding the restoration of human dignity, which had been totally violated during the colonial era. However, in many cases, the hopes ended in disappointment. The change of guards at Government House from white to black had not meant much in content. Violations of the individual's fundamental rights continued unabated.

In independent Africa, human rights issues were complicated by two major problems. First, while during the colonial period violations of rights of colonized people was seen and treated as a matter of international concern and debated heatedly in international forums, it was different in independent Africa. This time, human rights violations were reduced to a national affair and often kept from the eye of the international community by oversensitive governments. A second problem was created by the OAU Charter, newly adopted by the first leaders of independent Africa in Addis Ababa, Ethiopia, in May 1963. Article 3(ii) of this charter provides in clear terms that member states, in pursuit of the purposes of the organization, must adhere to, among other things, the principle of noninterference in the internal affairs of other states.(40) This seemingly innocent article, aimed at jealously protecting newly won sovereignty, became a subject of abuse over time. States could mishandle, torture, and even butcher their own citizens by the thousands with the rest of Africa watching helplessly. Any comment on these barbarian and inhuman acts by other African states would be interpreted as interference with the internal affairs of the state concerned.

In this context, the adoption of the African Charter on Human and People's Rights may be seen as a blow to certain regimes in Africa, namely those which had taken the noninterference clause in the OAU Charter as a license to violate the human rights of its citizens. Human rights violations in Africa are henceforth not only a matter of concern to Africans, but to the international community as a whole.(41)

There had been attempts before the adoption of the African Charter to address the issue of human rights in Africa. The First Conference of Independent African States was held at Accra, Ghana, April 15-22, 1958. At that time few African states were independent. Nonetheless, the meeting was held and, among other things, discussed the issue of human rights in Africa. In both its Declaration and Resolution, the conference affirmed the resolute adherence by African states to the principles enunciated at the Bandung Conference of Non-Aligned States, which included respect for fundamental human rights.(42)

Two years later, the Second Conference of Independent African States convened at Addis Ababa, June 15-29, 1960. The number of independent states in Africa was gradually increasing and human rights were gaining importance, especially in those territories still under foreign rule. This conference went on to characterize the subjugation of people to alien domination and exploitation as a denial of fundamental rights, which was contrary to both the Charter of the United Nations and the Universal Declaration of Human Rights.(43)

Another major conference in this early period was the Lagos Conference on Rule of Law in January 1961. This conference was organized and sponsored by the International Commission of Jurists--a nongovernmental organization specializing on the rule of law. Attended by about 200 participants, this conference included judges, practicing lawyers, and teachers of law from 23 African states, as well as nine countries of other continents. In its resolution, the conference proposed inter alia that personal liberty should be entrenched in the constitutions of all countries and that such personal liberties should not in peacetime be restricted without trial in a court of law.(44) It was also suggested that in order to give effect to the Universal Declaration of Human Rights, African governments should study the possibility of adopting an African Convention on Human Rights.(45)

The First Assembly of the Heads of State and Government of the OAU, meeting in Cairo in July 1964, made reference to human rights in its resolutions. Relevant to our discussion were the resolutions on racial discrimination in the United States and apartheid and racial discrimination in South Africa. In the latter resolution, the assembly called for the release from prison of Nelson Mandela, Walter Sisulu, the late Mangaliso Sobukwe, and all other nationalists imprisoned or detained under the arbitrary laws of South Africa.(46)

In the late 1950s and early 1960s the trend was to link the denial of fundamental human rights to colonialism. The reason is transparent. As indicated, under colonialism the degree of human rights violations had to concentrate on this inhumane system. A proper understanding of the reasons for the demand for respect of human rights in this early period is vital for the purposes of appreciating the new set of conditions giving rise to the outcry against violations of human rights in Africa in the 1970s.

The rise to power of dictators in Africa, just as elsewhere in the developing world, with the full support of imperialism during this period, contributed tremendously to the renewed call for respect of human rights. African governments have not tended to prepare for situations, but to react to them, some of which have become beyond control. Instead of preventing, they prefer to cure. Therefore, Africa experienced the regimes of Idi Amin in Uganda, Emperor Jean-Badel Bokassa in the Central African Republic, and Macias Nguema in Equatorial Guinea, to mention a few of the dictators who were killing hundreds of their subjects, day-in and day-out, before the OAU would react.(47)

Over the years, the OAU had developed what can only be
called an extremely insensitive attitude over events in
Africa. There was a lack of seriousness and interest in
penetrating to the heart of African problems. The naiveté
of the organization may be indicated by the holding of its
1975 summit meeting in Kampala, Uganda, thus making Idi
Amin Dada the chairman. The brutality of Amin's regime was
already an open secret. Only a few African states
boycotted the meeting. These were led by Botswana,
Mozambique, Tanzania, and Zambia. In its protest, the
government of Tanzania noted, among other things, that
"Africa is in danger of becoming unique in its refusal to
protest crimes committed against Africans, provided that
such actions are done by African leaders and African
governments."(48)

The fact that African leaders were pointing fingers at
the dictators did not mean they were innocent themselves or
that violations of human rights were restricted to the
dictators. Far from it. It has been suggested, in fact,
that the rise of the dictators was a gold mine for the
other African leaders who had, since independence, been
quietly mishandling political opponents.(49) The dictators
were a good cover for all to point to whenever human
rights issues were raised in Africa. In almost all African
states, there are detention laws allowing the state for any
obscure reason to detain without trial.(50) This blatant
violation of human rights is regarded as legal. As Kunig
correctly notes, "it used to be the colonizer who had to be
reminded of his declared support of human rights, but today
it is the black African critic of apartheid and colonialism
who is reproached with the defective state of enforcement
of human rights in his own country."(51)

Therefore, the accusation that African leaders are
pursuing double standards in the field of human rights may
be well-grounded.(52) Charity begins at home and to go by
the word of Mahalu, these African leaders should begin by
cleaning their own compounds first.(53)

The genesis of the current OAU Charter began with the
joint Senegal-Gambia resolution tabled at the Monrovia,
Liberia, summit meeting of the OAU in July 1979. The
resolution that was passed by the summit called for experts
to draft an African Charter on Human Rights.(54) To
implement the resolution, African experts gathered in
Dakar, Senegal, November 25-December 2, 1979, to prepare
the first draft of the proposed African Charter. The main
objective was to prepare a truly African convention on
human rights based on an African philosophy, and an
instrument that would be responsive to African needs.(55)
This objective was reemphasized and further stressed by the
former president of Senegal, Leopold Senghor, in his
address to the Dakar meeting of experts. He advised that
"as Africans, we shall neither copy, or strive for
originality. We must show imagination and effectiveness.
We could get inspirations from our beautiful and positive
traditions. Therefore, you must keep constantly in mind
our values of civilization and the real needs of
Africa."(56)

The OAU ministers of justice and legal experts met in

Banjul, the Gambia, June 8-15, 1980, to consider the draft charter. In this ministerial meeting, eleven articles were completed. The ministers met again in the same city January 7-19, 1981, to finalize the work of the charter. The final draft had 68 articles.(57)

On June 20, 1981, the draft charter was presented by then OAU Secretary General Edem Kodjo before the Plenary of the Council of Ministers in Nairobi.(58) The Council of Ministers noted the following points: (1) the draft charter left room for misinterpretation and, if adopted, could possibly conflict with the constitutions or laws of some member states; (2) article 45, which establishes the African Commission on Human and People's Rights, does not make clear that the commission does not have the authority to interfere with the internal affairs of the member states; (3) the charter does not protect certain rights, such as the right to independence and the right of women or wives,(59) nor does it sufficiently enumerate certain duties such as the respect due to the constitution, laws, and attributes of a state; and (4) the charter does not make it clear that the sole right of interpretation should be invested entirely with the Assembly of Heads of State and Government.(60)

Having debated the draft charter thoroughly, the Council of Ministers submitted it to the Assembly of Heads of State and Government for consideration, without making any amendments.

The 18th Assembly of Heads of State and Government adopted the charter as submitted after altering its name. The general feeling was that the name "African Charter on Human and People's Rights" could be easily confused with the "Charter of the Organization of African Unity." To avoid confusion, the term "African" was removed and replaced with "Banjul," the city in Gambia in which the document was drafted.

According to Article 63(2) of the charter, it would enter into force after ratification by a simple majority of the OAU member states. This has already been achieved. As indicated, the Banjul Charter came into force on October 21, 1986. Tanzania ratified the charter on May 31, 1982.(61) It is therefore bound by the charter and has a duty not only to implement the provisions of the charter that require implementation, but also to promote its aims, purposes, and objectives.

NOTES

1. Judge and former president of the International Court of Justice.

2. The Bill of Rights in Tanzania was introduced via the Fifth Amendment of the State Constitution of 1984 (Act No. 15 of 1984). It is now Section Three of the constitution, which has a total of 21 articles running from Articles 12 to 32. An unofficial English translation of the fifth amendment to the constitution prepared by the U.S. Embassy in Dar es Salaam is reproduced in Albert P. Blaustein and Gisbert H. Flanze (eds.), Constitutions of the Countries of the World, Volume XVII (Dobbs Ferry, N.Y.:

Oceana Publications, 1986.   These amendments have to be
read together with the Constitution of Tanzania, 1977,
which is reproduced in the 1979 release of the above cited
work.   See also R. M. Bierwagen and C. M. Peter, "The
Constitution of the United Republic of Tanzania: A Study of
the Fifth Amendment of 1984" (forthcoming).

    3. The African Charter on Human and People's Rights,
also sometimes referred to as the Banjul Charter on Human
and People's Rights, is reproduced in various internal
sources, including The Review of the International
Commission of Jurists, no. 27, December 1981 and
International Legal Materials 21 (1981), p. 58.

    4. See "African Charter in Force," Amnesty
International Newsletter, no. 12, December 1986, p.1.

    5. This is provided for in Section 5(2) of the
Constitution (Consequential, Transitional and Temporary
Provisions) Act, 1984 (Act No. 16 of 1984), which was
passed together with the Fifth Amendment Law.

    6. See Articles 19 to 24 of the African Charter on
Human and People's Rights.

    7. See J. S. Read, "Bill of Rights in the Third World,
Some Commonwealth Experiences," Verfassung und Recht in
Ubersee 6 (1973), p. 21.

    8. Tanzania was born in 1964 following the union
between Tanganyika and Zanzibar. The Articles of the Union
are reproduced in Michael F. Lofchie, Zanzibar: Background
to Revolution (Princeton: Princeton University Press,
1965), p. 285.

    9. The same argument was repeated in the proposals for
a republic a year after independence. See Proposals of the
Tanganyika Government for a Republic--Government Paper No.
1 of 1962. This paper is partly reproduced in Thomas
Franck, Human Rights in Third World Perspective, Volume 1
(Dobbs Ferry, N.Y.: Oceana Publications, 1982), p. 96.

    10. See Parliamentary Debates (Hansards), National
Assembly 3rd Meeting, 1088, 28 June 1962, quoted by L. T.
Kalunga, "Human Rights and the Preventive Detention Act,
1962, of the United Republic of Tanzania: Some Operative
Aspects," Eastern African Law Review 11-14 (1978-81), pp.
281-86.

    11. Robert Martin, Personal Freedom and the Law in
Tanzania (Nairobi: Oxford University Press, 1976), p. 40.
See also A. T. Nguluma, "The Right to Association in
Tanzania: Its Origin and Development" (mimeo.), a paper
presented at a seminar to commemorate 25 years of the
Faculty of Law of the University of Dar es Salaam in
October 1986.

    12. According to Cranford Pratt, the president chose
the commission in such a way that it would produce a
recommendation that would be of the sort he wanted. The
commission was chaired by Rashid Kawawa and included four
African Members of Parliament. Among them was Oscar
Kambona (then secretary-general of the party) (TANU), now
in self-imposed exile in England following a
misunderstanding with Nyerere allegedly due to the Arusha
Declaration, the expatriate Attorney-General Roland Brown,
Amon Nsekela (as secretary), four senior African civil
servants, and other Asian and European Members of
Parliament. See Pratt, The Critical Phase in Tanzania

1945-1968, p. 203.

13. See *Report of the Presidential Commission on Establishment of a Democratic One-Party State* (Dar es Salaam: Government Printer, 1968, p. 2, paragraph 8.   See also Julius Kambarage Nyerere, "Guide to the One-Party State Commission," in *Freedom and Unity* (Dar es Salaam: Oxford University Press, 1967), pp. 261-62.

14. The Interim Constitution of 1965 is reproduced in Kurt Rabl, "Constitutional Development and the Law of the United Republic of Tanzania: An Outline," *Jahrbuch des öffentlichen Rechts der Gegenwart* 16 (1967), pp. 567-610.

15. Court of Appeal of Tanzania at Arusha, Criminal Appeal No. 52 of 1979 and Criminal Appeal No. 53 of 1979. This case is treated at length in John Quigley, "Cases on Preventive Detention: A Review," *Eastern African Law Review* 11-14 (1978-81), p. 326.   For an earlier High Court decision on the status of the preamble, see *Hatimali Adamji vs. E.A.P.&T. Corporation*, (1973) Law Reports of Tanzania No. 6.

16. See Article 2 of the Constitution of the Tanganyika African National Union (TANU), which is a schedule to the Interim Constitution of 1965.   See Rabl, "Constitutional Development and the Law of the United Republic of Tanzania, p. 628.

17. (1973) Law Reports of Tanzania No. 24.

18. The Constitution of the United Republic of Tanzania plus the Fifth Amendment are reproduced in Blaustein and Flanz (eds.), *Constitutions of the Countries of the World*.

19. On how the office of the Ombudsman works, see Niall MacDermot, "The Ombudsman Institution," *The Review of International Commission of Jurists*, 21, December 1978, p. 37.

20. See Chapter VI of the Interim Constitution of 1965, which comprises Articles 67, 68, and 69.

21. See the analysis of the commission powers in the following works: J. P. W. B. McAuslan and Yash P. Ghai, "Constitutional Innovation and Political Stability in Tanzania: A Preliminary Assessment," *Journal of Modern African Studies* 4, No. 4 (1966), pp. 474-502; Patrick M. Norton, "The Tanzanian Ombudsman," *The International and Comparative Law Quarterly* 22 (1973), p. 603; Peter Oluyede, "Redress of Grievances in Tanzania," *Public Law* (1975), p. 8; and Kent M. Weeks, *Ombudsman Around the World: A Comparative Chart* (Berkeley: Institute of Governmental Studies, 1978), p. 110.

22. Act No. 25 of 1966.   In the Constitution of the United Republic of Tanzania, 1977, the Permanent Commission of Enquiry is provided for under Chapter VI Section 1 (Articles 129, 130, and 131).

23. Article 67(1) of the Interim Constitution, 1965.

24. Article 67(4) of the Interim Constitution, 1965.

25. Ibid.

26. Article 67(5) of the Interim Constitution, 1965.

27. Article 68 of the Interim Constitution, 1965 and McAuslan and Ghai, "Constitutional Innovation and Political Stability in Tanzania, p. 504.

28. See Samuel K. B. Asante, "National Building and Human Rights in Emergent African Nations," Cornell International Law Journal 2 (1969), pp. 72-80.

29. See Chama Cha Mapinduzi, 1983 NEC Proposals for Changes in the Constitution of the United Republic and the Constitution of the Revolutionary Government of Zanzibar (Dodoma: CCM, Department of Propaganda and Mass Mobilization, 1983).

30. Some of the papers presented in this seminar by the Tanganyika Law Society, held in July 1983, are published in Eastern African Law Review 11-14 (1978-81), a cumulative edition that appeared in 1985.

31. See Chapter II of the Constitution of the State of Zanzibar, titled "Protection of Fundamental Rights and Freedoms of the Individual" (Articles 14-31). This constitution is reproduced in Bill Supplement to the Official Gazette Extraordinary of the Zanzibar Government, Volume LXXII, No. 4315, November 14, 1963.

32. See Section 2(2) of Presidential Decree No. 1 of 1964, which is reproduced in Legal Supplement (Part 1) to the Zanzibar Gazette Extraordinary, Volume LXXIII, No. 4344, March 2, 1964, p. 1. This decree has to be read together with General Notice No. 73 of 1964.

33. See Presidential Decree No. 5 of 1964 titled "Constitutional Decree Providing for Constitutional Government and the Rule of Law." See Legal Supplement (Part 1) to the Zanzibar Gazette Extraordinary, Volume LXXIII, No. 4344, March 2, 1964, p. 9.

34. This was done through the Preventive Detention Decree, 1964, which was Presidential Decree No. 3 of 1964. See Legal Supplement (Part 1) to the Zanzibar Gazette Extraordinary, Volume LXXIII, No. 4344, March 2, 1964, p. 5.

35. Confiscation of immovable property was done through Presidential Decree No. 8 of 1964, which made provision for the confiscation of immovable property in certain cases. This decree is reproduced in Legal Supplement (Part 1) to the Zanzibar Gazette Extraordinary, Volume LXXIII, No. 4347, March 21, 1964, p. 15.

36. See Presidential Decree No. 23 of 1964, which restricted the taking of legal proceedings with respect to certain acts and matters done between January 12 and February 12, 1964, and certain claims and for matters indicated above. This was one month after the revolution that resulted in considerable damage to property and to life. For this decree, see Legal Supplement (Part 1) to the Zanzibar Gazette Extraordinary, Volume LXXIII, No. 4390, December 12, 1964.

37. On this shocking event, see Ivison Macadam (ed.), The Annual Register: World Events in 1970 (London: Longman Group, 1971), p. 218.

38. One of the women involved was later adopted by Amnesty International as a prisoner of conscience in 1979. She was Nasreen Mohamed Hussein, who had been forced to marry a security officer, Ali Foum Kimara, with whom she had four children; but notwithstanding, had not accepted her situation. See Amnesty International, Jahresbericht 1979 (Frankfurt: Fischer Taschenbuch Verlag, 1980), pp. 62-63. Due to pressure from various parts of the world, she

was later allowed to leave Zanzibar and join her family, which was exiled in 1981. See Amnesty International, Jahresbericht 1981 (Frankfurt: Fischer Taschenbuch Verlag, 1982), p. 118.

39. It is actually alleged that it is Zanzibaris within the party who engineered the fall from power of Aboud Jumbe.

40. See the Charter of the Organization of African Unity which is reproduced in full in International Legal Materials 2, No. 3 (1963), p. 766.

41. See Edward Kannyo, "The Banjul Charter on Human and People's Rights: Genesis and Political Background," in Claude E. Welch, Jr., and Ronald I. Meltzer (eds.), Human Rights and Development in Africa (Albany: State University of New York Press, 1984), p. 128.

42. Apart from the declaration, the conference passed resolutions on exchange of views on foreign policy, the future of the dependent territories in Africa, and racism. For the texts of these resolutions, see Ian Brownlie, Basic Documents on Human Rights (Oxford: Clarendon, 1981), pp. 418-21.

43. See the Resolution on Eradication of Colonial Rule for Africa. Other resolutions adopted by the same 2nd Conference of Independent African States, 1960, were on Eradication of Colonial Rule from Africa, Means to Prevent New Forms of Colonialism in Africa, and Policy of Apartheid and Racial Discrimination in Africa. See Brownlie, Basic Documents on Human Rights, pp. 422-25.

44. See the resolution of the conference: The Law of Lagos Article 3. The conference was divided into three separate committees, each of which prepared written conclusions. These committees were on (1) human rights and government security--the judiciary, legislative and executive; (2) human rights and aspects of criminal and administrative law; and (3) the responsibility of the judiciary and the bar for the protection of the rights of the individual in the society.

For the texts of the resolution of the conference and the conclusions of the committees, see Brownlie, Basic Documents on Human Rights, pp. 426-32.

45. Ibid.

46. For the text of the resolutions of the First Assembly of the Heads of State and Government of the OAU, 1964, see Brownlie, Basic Documents on Human Rights, pp. 435-37.

47. See George Ayittey, "African Freedom of Speech," Index on Censorship 16(1) January 1987, p. 16. See also Semakula Kiwanuka, Amin and the Tragedy of Uganda (Munich: Weltforum Verlag, 1979), David Martin, General Amin (London: Faber and Faber, 1974), and Mohamood Mamdani, Imperialism and Fascism in Uganda (Nairobi: Heinemann Educational Books, 1983).

48. This statement, issued on July 25, 1975 by the Tanzanian Ministry of Information and Broadcasting, is quoted in Claude E. Welch, Jr., "The OAU and Human Rights: Towards a New Definition," Journal of Modern African Studies 19, No. 3 (1981), pp. 401-405.

49. See Ayittey, "African Freedom of Speech."

50. For detention laws in Africa, see Preventive
Detention Act, 1962, Chapter 490 of the Laws (Act No. 60 of
1962) (Tanzania), Preventive Detention Act, 1958 (Act No.
17 of 1958) (Ghana), Preservation of Public Security
Regulations made under Chapter 106 of the Laws (Zambia),
Emergency Powers Act, 1961 (Nigeria), the Preservation of
Public Security Act, 1966 (Act No. 18 of 1966) (Kenya), and
Law No. 2/71 of July 26, 1971 amending the Code of Military
Justice (Morocco).

51. See Philip Kunig, "The Protection of Human Rights
by International Law in Africa," German Yearbook of
International Law 25 (1982), pp. 138-39.

52. See Cost Ricky Mahalu, "Africa and Human Rights,"
in Philip Kunig, Wolfgang Benedek, and Costa Ricky Mahalu
(eds.), Regional Protection of Human Rights by International Law: The Emerging African System (Baden-Baden:
Nomos Verlagsgesellschaft, 1985), pp. 1-14.

53. Ibid., p. 15.

54. OAU Document AHG/115 (XVI) of the Monrovia summit
meeting held in July 1979.

55. See OAU Document CAB/LEG/67/3/Rev.1.

56. The address by then president of Senegal Leopold
Senghor on November 28, 1979 to the Dakar meeting of
experts preparing the draft African Charter on Human and
People's Rights (OAU Document CAB/LEG/67/X, p.6) is
reproduced in Kunig, Benedek, and Mahalu, Regional
Protection of Human Rights by International Law: The
Emerging African System, p. 121.

57. See OAU Document CAB/LEG/67/3/Rev.5.

58. See the Report of the Secretary-General on the
African Charter on Human and People's Rights--OAU Document
CM/1149/XXXVII (1981).

59. It is unfortunate that there was no follow-up on
this point. Women constitute more than half of the African
continent's population and there are specific human rights
issues that directly touch African women. They range from
denial of the right to property to such oppressive
cultural rituals as circumcision, which deprives them not
only of one of their most sensitive parts, but also their
natural rights to sexuality. It has been forcefully
argued that this is an affront to a woman's human rights
and dignity. See the research by Asma El Dareer titled
"Women, Why do You Weep? Circumcision and Its Consequences," quoted at length in William J. House, "The
Status of Women in the Sudan," Journal of Modern African
Studies 26, No. 2 (1988), p. 300.

60. See Diary No. 6, June 21, 1981, p. 1. See also
Document CM/Plen. Draft Rapt. Rep. (XXXVII) (1981), p. 60.
Also the introductory note by Richard Gittleman of the
International Human Rights Law Group, Washington, D.C., in
International Legal Materials (1982), p. 58.

61. See Amnesty International, Jahresbericht 1983
(Frankfurt: Fischer Taschenbuch Verlag, 1983), p. 119.

Chapter 2
The Tanzanian Bill of Rights and the Banjul Charter on Human and People's Rights: A Comparison

As explained in chapter 1, these two documents are different in terms of authorship and also as far as the audiences are concerned. One is by a parliament of a sovereign state and addressed to all citizens and the other is by a continental organization and addressed to the signatory member states. While the first forms part of the national law of the country concerned, the other forms part of regional international law. These differences make it nearly impossible to find exact similarities in the formulation of rights, freedoms, and duties in the two documents. Therefore, it will be necessary to draw implications from interpretation of various provisions where important points have not been explicitly made. Also, where data and information allow, we shall venture into the historical reasons and refer to incidences connected to and relevant to particular rights, freedoms, duties, or obligations.

RIGHTS AND FREEDOMS

Right to Equality

Equality of all human beings is one of the most important if not the basic human right. It is therefore not accidental that it was placed in Article One of the Universal Declaration of Human Rights of 1948. This article is worth reciting. It provides that:

> All human beings are born free and equal in dignity and rights. They are endowed with reason and conscience and should act towards one another in a spirit of brotherhood.(1)

This right has wide-ranging implications. It means that no human being should be regarded as inferior due to race, ethnic group, sex, language, religion, or political or other opinions. Therefore, social status, wealth, nationality, class and similar attributes should never be taken as criteria for grading human beings. This is a

right against all forms of discrimination. Both the
Banjul Charter and the Tanzanian Bill of Rights recognize
and provide for this right.(2) Certain principles have
been developed to make this right a reality. Among these
is the provision of equal rights before the law. This
principle has been underlined in the two documents under
discussion. The Banjul Charter is brief and general on this
issue, while the Tanzania Bill of Rights is elaborate.(3)
The latter forbids certain practices by the agencies of the
state which limit the quality of the parties before the
law. It is, for instance, forbidden for anyone to
discriminate on any basis in exercise of power under any
law or carrying out any duty or function of authority of
state or the party and its organs.(4) That is a general
prohibition on any type of discrimination.

Then there are specific forms of conduct which are
also prohibited since they may limit the realization of the
right to equality before the law. In criminal law and
procedure, for instance, it is forbidden to consider
accused persons guilty of the offense they are charged with
until they have been proven guilty of that offense.(5)
This is a reenactment of one of the major rules of natural
justice. Therefore, before people can be declared guilty
there must be inquiries in which the accused are clearly
informed of the accusations preferred against them and
afforded the opportunity of being heard.(6) It is an
important rule in the law of evidence that offenses have to
be proved. Here standards have been set: proof is
required "on balance of probabilities" and "beyond
reasonable doubts" on lighter and serious allegations,
respectively. The law on detention without trial, which we
shall treat at length later in connection with freedom of
movement, is a major hindrance to the right to be
considered innocent until the contrary is proved.

It is also forbidden to torture or otherwise punish
excessively or to mete out punishment that humiliates or
degrades a person.(7) This provision was actually
addressed to the police and security forces who in
execution of their duties commit unusual and terrible
crimes against humanity. This is usually done in the
process of interrogation of alleged criminals. In
Tanzania, this provision is more than timely, as there have
been many reported cases of torture and mishandling of
persons in custody. Among these cases is that of James
Nagoti, a former manager of the Currency Department in the
Central Bank of Tanzania.(8) Nagoti was arrested in
connection with the theft of huge sums of money from the
bank in November 1976. In the process of interrogation by
members of the security forces a series of inhumane and
degrading methods were applied by his interrogators. These
included forcing bottles into his anus, burning his
genitals with lighted cigarettes, and application of
electric shocks on various sensitive parts of his body. As
a result of this severe torture he became impotent.
Shocking evidence was given in the trial of the two
security officers who tortured him. In spite of the
gravity of their offense, the two officers got away with a
light sentence of three years in jail each in July
1978.(9)

Torture by security forces was also reported in the Mwanza and Shinyanga regions in 1976. In these two regions, the security agents arrested and tortured (in some cases leading to death) persons suspected of murder who were rumored to be "witches" and alleged to be the cause of a series of unresolved murders in the two regions. The president of Tanzania at the time, Julius K. Nyerere, appointed a commission of inquiry to investigate the allegations against the security forces' behavior. When the commission's findings were received showing that maltreatment of citizens had occurred, two cabinet ministers resigned. These were the current president of Tanzania, Ali Hassan Mwinyi, who was then Minister of Home Affairs, and Peter Siyovelwa, then Minister of State in the resident's office responsible for security affairs. Also to resign were the Regional Commissioners of the two regions, Marco Mabawa (Shinyanga) and Peter Abdallah Kisumo (Mwanza).(10) Although the four politicians were not in any way directly involved in the tortures or maltreatment of the suspects, they offered to resign as acceptance of responsibility for the actions of junior police and other officers in their departments. Nyerere accepted the resignations "with a heavy heart, in order to establish the principle of political responsibility in the country."(11) It is no wonder therefore that he later offered them other jobs elsewhere in the establishment. The security officers involved in the direction of the torture in these two regions were later prosecuted and convicted by law courts. They were given jail sentences ranging from five to fifteen years.(12)

Equality before the law also means that one can be punished only for breach of an existing law. In recognition of this old and known rule, the Tanzanian Bill of Rights forbids punishing for any action which at the time of its commission was not an offense under the law.(13) This provision enacts the maxim <u>nullum crimen sine lege, nulla poena sine lege</u>, a presumption that citizens should be guided in their behavior by pre-announced rules which can be ascertained with due diligence.(14) The effect of this rule is to make it impossible for the state to enact retroactive laws. In Tanzania, the government is known for opting out of the law into illegality in order to attempt to halt a deteriorating situation. Many retroactive laws have been enacted in the country which criminalize actions which were not crimes when committed. An example is the Economic Sabotage (Special Provisions) Act, 1983. This act, which, among other things, completely excluded the jurisdiction of the normal courts of law in dealing with the so-called economic offenses, was enacted in April 1983 but was proclaimed to have come into effect on March 24, 1983. It had to be pushed two months back in order to cover cases of persons who had already been illegally arrested and were languishing in custody. This law, which has been correctly characterized as "a Draconian piece of legislation," has now been repealed and replaced by the Economic and Organized Crime Control Act, 1984.(15) The new law, which allows bail to the accused and opens the way to the normal courts of law, was enacted mainly due to

heavy criticism and public outcry.   Many other   pieces of
legislation have been enacted in this fashion to meet
political ends.

Right to Life

The right to life has two main parts.   First, it
refers to the right of the protection of the physical body
against external aggression which threatens to extinguish
life itself.   Second, it is the protection of life through
the nourishment of the body.   Both the Banjul Charter and
the Tanzanian Bill of Rights refer to this important
right.(16) This right is derived from the   common African
tradition that   society has   a duty   to protect its members
against attack and also to provide the means of survival to
those without   the basic essentials to ensure normal
subsistence.(17)
According to the Banjul Charter, the right to life can
be ensured through inviolability of the person and respect
of the dignity, liberty, and security of the person. The
Tanzanian Bill of Rights specifically mentions conduct by
the state which amounts to infringement of the right to
life.   These include illegal arrest, remand, detention, or
repatriation of a person.   In the 1970s and 1980s there
have been many reported violations of the right of the
individual to life. Mainly these have to do with detention
of persons already declared innocent by courts of law. A
classic example is the case of <u>Lesinoi Ndeinai or Joseph
Selayo Laizer and Masai Lekasi vs. Regional Prisons Officer
and Regional Police Commander</u>.(18) In this case, the two
plaintiffs were arrested in August 1979, pursuant to the
orders of the officer commanding the district. From police
custody they were transferred to prison with no charges
being preferred against them.   Naturally wanting to be
free, they filed for habeas corpus, which the High Court
granted, ordering their immediate release.   However, the
unexpected happened.   On stepping outside the courtroom as
free men, the two were immediately rearrested and returned
to prison.   The   order of the court that they be released,
as their detention was illegal, was totally ignored and
disobeyed by both the police and the prison officers.
Incidents of this nature are not rare in Tanzania.(19)
It exposes the life of a person to danger if a
government repatriates a person to a country where he or
she is wanted, particularly for political reasons.   The
basis of the law on asylum is basically to protect
endangered persons.(20) It is interesting, therefore, to
see the way Tanzania deals with the issue of repatriation.
For a long time Tanzania was regarded as the safest place
for persons running away from persecution in their own
countries.   It has therefore hosted many refugees and
freedom fighters, especially from countries still under
colonial and racist regimes.
This good record is marred by a tendency which has
developed between Tanzania and its neighbors to enter into
illegal secret pacts whereby persons sought in each others'
territory are arrested and repatriated by force or
exchanged.   The first of these pacts was entered into in

1962, just a year after independence. This was with respect to Christopher Tumbo, a trade unionist and member of parliament who had left Tanzania (then Tanganyika) in 1962 in order to avoid detention. He had lived and worked in Mombasa, Kenya, and used to make critical comments on Tanzanian affairs. Irritated by his comments, the government of Tanzania secured the cooperation of the Kenya police, who kidnapped him and transported him to a Tanzanian border post, where he was arrested and detained.(21)

As recently as 1983, against all norms of international law, the governments of Tanzania and Kenya extradited persons wanted in each others' territories in connection with coup attempts. The Tanzanians returned by Kenya included Hatty McGhee, a pilot formerly with the Air Tanzanian Corporation who had escaped from remand prison while awaiting a treason trial,(22) and Saidi Lamke, a businessman who had for a long time lived in Kenya and had already been granted Kenyan citizenship.(23) Tanzania, on its part, extradited among others the alleged leader of the unsuccessful coup of August 1, 1982, in Kenya, Hezekiah Ochuka. The extradited Kenyans were brought before a court martial, charged with treason, and condemned to death. Their execution was carried out secretly at the notorious Kamiti Maximum Security Prison, Nairobi.(24) This exchange of political refugees, which is said to have speeded up the opening of the border between the two countries, closed since 1977, raised serious concerns in institutions dealing with human rights and particularly the United Nations.(25) One can only hope that with the Bill of Rights coming into force, the government will have second thoughts before indulging in similar acts in the future.

Freedom of Movement

Restriction of freedom of movement is felt more than infringement of other rights because the exercise of this freedom involves almost everyone. In principle, one should be able to move as freely as one likes without restriction. However, at times, restrictions have been introduced mainly in realization of the fact that individuals are part of the society in which they live. Therefore, in exercise of various freedoms, including that of movement, one ought to take into account the fact that the rights of other human beings also have to be respected.

The Banjul Charter, in advocating freedom of movement, adds a small clause that this freedom has to be exercised subject to the individual abiding by the law.(26) This is a general condition which is not problematic. However, there are situations where the exceptions to the rule become more relevant than the rule itself. Specifically, in some situations the set of restrictions to this freedom are so many that they make the freedom itself unrealizable. Such is the situation created by the new Bill of Rights in Tanzania. It provides freedom of movement with the right hand and takes it away with the left. Article 17(1) of the constitution provides for this freedom and immediately thereafter Article 17(2) provides for ways in which the state can legally and with impunity restrict that freedom.   The government can enact laws to: diminish the freedom of people to go wherever they wish; put them under guard or in prison; establish boundaries for the freedom of people to go wherever they want pursuant to carrying out the judgment of any court order or to complete first any obligations expected of them--to restrict their freedom of movement for the purposes of protecting national interest can rarely be justified. Taken in their totality, the above can mean only one thing, that there is no general presumption of freedom of movement in Tanzania.

This somewhat stark assertion is supported by citing laws which actually or potentially restrict this freedom. A survey of some of these will illustrate the point.   To begin with, a penal code that was enacted during the colonial period is not only still intact, but has been amended from time to time to enforce its utility.(27) Among the most oppressive sections of the penal code is Section 176.   This section refers to a category of persons regarded as "idle and disorderly persons." Among these are prostitutes, beggars, gamblers, pimps, and similar persons. The police and other law enforcing agents of the state can arrest any person who seems "idle and disorderly." The penalty on conviction is harsh and on second conviction such a person is declared a "rogue and vagabond" and the penalty rises.

We have referred to the above section because of a dramatic amendment to it made in 1983 which increased by two the existing seven categories of "idle and disorderly persons."   The new categories are (1) any able-bodied person who is not engaged in any productive work and has no visible means of subsistence; and (2) any person employed under lawful employment of any description who is, without any lawful excuse, found engaged in an enterprise of his own at a time he is supposed to be engaged in activities connected or related to the business of his employment.

Apart from restricting the individual's right to movement, the above amendment encroaches on another fundamental right of the individual, namely the freedom of contract. Absence from duty for reasons unconnected with employment is at most a disciplinary offense which is actually one of the breaches of the contract of employment. This is a civil wrong and within relations between the employer and the employee. Remedy for breaches of contract can lie only in civil law and not in penal law. This government amendment of the penal code to penalize civil relations is both misplaced and extremely oppressive.

More serious restriction of movement of the individual is through detention without trial and restriction of an individual's movement to a given district or region. Detention without trial means imprisonment of an individual without guilt having been proven before a court of law. A victim of this type of imprisonment is usually a suspect whose conduct and acts are alleged to be prejudicial or dangerous to the security of the state. Many states, not only in Africa and the developing world, have such laws on their statute books.(28)   The difference lies in nomenclature but the purpose is the same. Detention laws are, strictly speaking, meant to deal with political crimes aimed at subverting the state. However, there are times when detention has been used as a tool for silencing political opponents and general dissent.

Tanzania has a law on detention without trial. This law, the Tanganyika Preventive Detention Act, 1962, was enacted just a year after independence.(29) This legislation empowers the president to detain any person whose conduct endangers peace and order in any part of Tanganyika or who acts in a manner prejudicial to the defense of Tanganyika or the security of the state. Where such a detention has been ordered by the president under his hand and the public seal, it cannot be questioned in any court of law.

Politicians have often attempted not only to defend this law but to justify its existence. They argue that it is a necessary evil. For instance, Nyerere, former president of Tanzania, while inaugurating the University College, Dar es Salaam, argued strongly for the detention law in his usual articulate manner:

> Take the question of detention without trial. This is a desperately serious matter. It means that you are imprisoning a man when he has not broken any written law, when you cannot be sure of proving beyond reasonable doubt that he has done so. You are restricting his liberty and making him suffer materially and spiritually for what you think he intends to do, or is trying to do, or for what you believe he has done. Few things are more dangerous to the freedom of a society than that. For freedom is indivisible, and with such an opportunity open to the government of the day, the freedom of every citizen is reduced. To suspend the rule of law under any circumstance is to leave open the possibility of the grossest injustices being perpetrated.
>
> Yet, knowing these things, I have still supported the introduction of a law which gives the government power to detain people without trial. I have myself signed Detention Orders. I have done these things in an inevitable part of my responsibilities as president of the Republic. For in even so important and fundamental an issue as this, other principles conflict. Our union has neither the long tradition of nationhood, nor the strong physical means of national security, which older countries take for granted. While the vast mass of the people give full and active support to their country and its government, a handful of individuals can still put our nation into jeopardy and reduce to ashes the efforts of millions.(30)

One wonders if such justification still holds more than a quarter of a century after independence. Yet, the detention law is in full application.(31) Apart from a few cosmetic changes, the Preventive Detention Act is still intact as it was originally framed. The only notable change came in 1985 through the Preventive Detention

(Amendment) Act, 1985, which amended Section 3 in order to allow challenging the legality of a detention on any ground in the courts of law. The same amendment legislation, however, did the disservice of extending the application of the Preventive Detention Act to Zanzibar, which had not been covered before. The original detention law referred to Tanganyika and thus applied only to mainland Tanzania.(32)

To supplement the Preventive Detention Act, the government often applies the Deportation Ordinance.(33) This law, enacted by the British during the colonial era, empowers the president to deport people from one part of the republic to another and restrict them to the place of deportation. This law is usually invoked when it comes to dealing with strong political opponents who are popular with the masses. Such persons are deported to remote areas in the country, removed from their political bases in order to undermine and quietly kill their popularity. An example is the case of Victor Mkello, a popular labor leader during the independence struggle. Mkello, who was president of both the Plantation Workers Association and the Tanganyika Federation of Labor (TFL) was, together with Sheshe Amiri, the acting secretary of the Plantation Workers Association, restricted to a settlement on the Zambian border.(34)

To ensure the presence of the deportee in the place of deportation, the authorities instruct that the deportee should report to the police or party functionaries at regular intervals--perhaps once a week. There are times when the authorities have exceeded their authority in connection with this legislation. The law applies only to mainland Tanzania. However, people have been deported from the mainland to Zanzibar in total disregard of the provisions of the law. This happened, for example, in the case of Sheikh Mohamed Nassoro Abdallah vs. the Regional Police Commander, Dar es Salaam.(35)   In this case, a religious leader was arrested at his house at Mabibo in Dar es Salaam and whisked away under police custody and was later deported to Zanzibar on the order of the president. This deportation was challenged in the High Court on the ground that the president has no power under the Deportation Ordinance to deport a person from any part of Tanganyika to Zanzibar and thus, by deporting the applicant, the president had exceeded his powers. The High Court upheld the application and issued the order of habeas corpus. However, as usual, the authorities ignored the court order and the applicant is still restricted in Zanzibar.

Worse still, this ordinance provides that while awaiting the deportation formalities to be finalized, the deportee is to be held in custody. This provision has been a subject of excessive abuse by the police. Typically, once the deportee is in their custody, they take their time in the so-called "finalization" of the deportation formalities. In some cases, it has taken more than a year before the deportee eventually arrives at the place of deportation. All this time, the deportee, who has committed no cognizable offense and who, after all, is not supposed to be physically detained in the place of deportation, languishes in prison like a criminal.

There are other laws which restrict the individual's
freedom of movement.   These include the Expulsion of
Undesirables Ordinance,   1930;(36) the Resettlement of
Offenders Act, 1969;(37) Human Resources Deployment Act,
1983;(38) Rural Lands (Planning and Utilization) Act, 1973;
(39)   Area   Commissioners   Act,   1962;   and   Regional
Commissioners Act, 1962.(40)   Interesting among these is
the Witchcraft Ordinance.(41)   This ordinance allows
administrative officers to order persons suspected of
practicing witchcraft to reside in certain places.(42)
This power has been used, for example, to detain 30
Wanyambuda in Mbeya District who were allegedly influencing
people by the use of witchcraft not to join Ujamaa
villages.(43) The most recent piece of legislation which
totally blocks the individual's freedom of movement within
the country is the Registration and Identification of
Persons Act, 1986.(44)   The object of this act is to
provide for the registration of all persons in the United
Republic of Tanzania and the issuance of identity cards.
This may seem a very noble and well-intended objective. It
is only after careful examination of the act that one
finds quite objectionable, if not repugnant, provisions.
     According to Section 7 of this act, all persons
resident in Tanzania, both citizens and aliens, are
supposed to register and be issued identity cards.   The
act goes on to provide, in Section 10(1), that all people
issued an identity card shall carry the card on their
person at all times.   Section 20(1)(a) specifically
provides that it is an offense to fail to carry or refuse
to register an identity card.   Scholars have commented
that this law finds parallel only in the Pass Laws of South
Africa and have characterized the compulsion to carry the
identity card everywhere one goes as an unnecessary evil.
It is not therefore surprising that this act was marginally
passed by the parliament after a long and heated debate and
extensive amendments.   Attempts to enforce this law shall
be inconsistent with the provisions of Article 17 of the
constitution.(45)
     All in all, these laws and many others restrict the
freedom of citizens to move as they like in their own
country contrary to all international conventions, which
call for provision and assurance of such a right.
     Over and above the laws, there is a cluster of
baseless Executive Regulations which also interfere with
freedom of movement. The most notorious among these is the
so-called State House Clearance. This regulation, which
has now also been introduced in neighboring Kenya, requires
citizens wishing to travel out of the country to seek and
obtain a clearance from the State House through their
employers or other agencies, such as the party, if self-
employed.(46)
     This clearance is so important that travel formalities
cannot begin without it.   The Central Bank is not allowed
to issue foreign currency to an applicant who does not have
such a clearance.   In turn, issuance of this clearance is
at the total discretion of some officers in the State
House.   It can be granted or refused without reasons being
stated.   This regulation, which has been in effect for
years now, has, however, never been challenged in a court

of law to test its legality. Nevertheless, it ought to be removed.

Freedom of Expression

Freedom of expression consists of the guarantee of two basic rights: the right to express and disseminate opinions in any form and the right to freely receive information from any source without restriction. The Banjul Charter provides for freedom of expression in Article 9. This article simply says that it is the right of every individual to receive information and disseminate opinions. The Bill of Rights in Tanzania is more elaborate on this freedom.(47) It provides that each and every person has the right to freely express any opinion and search for and receive information and any ideas through any medium without consideration of country of origin. In furtherance of this right, the constitution guarantees the right to personal communication without interference. Furthermore, the individual has the right of being informed on different events taking place in the country and the world. Of course, this right goes hand-in-hand with the usual clause that it is to be enjoyed subject to the laws of the country.

The authors of this Bill of Rights were conscious of the fact that there is a tendency to be myopic and parochial on the part of some regimes. Information is power. Therefore, these regimes tailor the education and the information dissemination system in general in such a way that the world begins and ends in that particular country. Apart from the normal business advertisement, all the citizen is informed about is what the president has done or said, and nothing about the world.

Also, the Bill of Rights takes cognizance of the censorship and doctoring of information. Many countries impose serious censorship on information that is allowed to the population. This includes restriction of literature coming from certain parts of the world and in particular works based on ideological information not favored by the authorities. It is for this reason that it is specifically provided that information can be received from anywhere without consideration of country.

Many things are more easily said than practiced. Theoretically, freedom of expression is supposed to exist in Tanzania. On many occasions, politicians have made it a point to remind the citizens of their right to speak their minds. In 1966, President Nyerere, in a speech on Mafia Island, told attentive peasants:

> This is your country. We tell you every day that you have freedom of speech. If you do not accept your responsibility for this country I shall claim ownership of it. Any country must be looked after by people. If you do not accept the responsibility of looking after this country, I shall get a few clever people and together we will declare this country to be our property...If we do not remove fear from our people and if we do not abolish the two classes of

masters and servants from our society, clever people
will emerge from among us to take the place of
Europeans, Indians, and Arabs. These clever people
will continue to exploit our fear for their own
benefit. And we leaders can become the clever
people...this is going to happen if you do not remove
fear from your minds.(48)

That is what is called "double talk." It is true that
generally people feel free to discuss various issues, some
of them extremely sensitive, in open places like markets,
buses, etc. This is different from other countries where
security forces and plainclothes police haunt the masses to
the level of total submission. There comes a time when
people are afraid of their own shadows.
In Tanzania, the government and the party have
systematically taken control of all forms of public
communication. In other words, the state is in full
control of the so-called ideological apparatus. There are
only two dailies in the country. One, in English, called
the Daily News, is owned by the government, and the other,
Uhuru (freedom or independence), in Kiswahili, is owned
and controlled by the ruling party--Chama Cha Mapinduzi.
There are two radio stations, Radio Tanzania, Dar es
Salaam, on the mainland and Sauti ya Tanzania, Zanzibar.
These two and the color television station in Zanzibar are
all owned by the governments of Tanzania and Zanzibar.(49)
There are a few weekly and monthly newspapers and magazines
published by government departments, public institutions,
or religious bodies. These are usually specialized and
stick to certain fields and shy away from politics.
Nonetheless, they are under the careful eye of the
government. Every issue of these publications has to be
sanctioned by the ministry responsible for information and
broadcasting before coming out on the streets.
More restrictions were imposed in 1976 with the
formation of the Tanzania News Agency (Shirika la Habari
Tanzania--SHIHATA).(50) This institution, which is a
corporate body, is the only one in the whole country with
the right to collect and distribute news. Any person
intending to work in any business connected with news
gathering or distribution, such as free-lance journalists,
photographers, or correspondents, has to be authorized by
SHIHATA. Such authorization has to be paid for. A recent
rise in fees payable by journalists to SHIHATA caused an
international outcry.(51) The presence of SHIHATA has been
attacked in various discussions in Tanzania as a
governmental method of suppressing freedom of expression in
the country. It has been argued that such a restriction
leads to rumor-mongering as there is no credible source of
information for the public.(52) In his very apologetic and
progovernment book on press freedom in Tanzania, Hadji
Konde,(53) a former director of SHIHATA, argues that there
is freedom of the press in the country, but in the same
book goes on to narrate various instances of total
harassment of the mass media personnel by all sorts of
persons, ranging from police and security personnel to
District Commissioners and party functionaries.(54)
At the same time, the government, apart from ensuring

tight control on dissemination of information through ownership of the various forms of news media, makes it a point to discourage or kill every initiative for creative journalism in either the radio or the newspapers. Any newspaper column or radio program which is based on investigation and seems critical to the establishment is quietly but unceremoniously silenced.(55)   If it is too popular, then it is diluted by appointing a pro-establishment person to run it so as to deal with nonissues. It has been said that to survive in the media in Tanzania one has to be mediocre, as there mediocrity excels and excellence despairs.(56)

Therefore, if the Bill of Rights is to have any meaning, the government must relax this quiet censorship of information and allow more private initiative in the communications industry.   This should force government agencies to wake up and compete, rather than merely parrot government and party statements daily without objectivity or analysis. This should also create variety for the very literate Tanzanian population.(57)

Freedom of Worship

Freedom of worship is closely related to freedom of expression and freedom of peaceful assembly.   The Banjul Charter combines the freedom of the practice of religion with that of conscience and profession.(58)   The Tanzanian Bill of Rights declares the entitlement of every individual to freedom of thought, worship, and choice on matters of religion.(59)   The Bill of Rights goes on to separate the administration of religion from the jurisdiction of the state.(60)   Promotion of religion, worship, and evangelization are taken as private matters.

The separation of religion from the state is important if freedom of worship is to be realized. In some countries there is a total union between the state and the means of worship, while in others there is what are called state religions. For example, in many Arab countries, Islam is declared a state religion and religious law, i.e., Sharia, applies to all. In other states, a state religion extends even to the level of finances and the income of the individual.   In the Federal Republic of Germany, for instance, every citizen has a duty to pay a given percentage of his/her yearly income to his/her church. This is compulsory, except where a person has formally renounced religion.(61)   Actually, the church tax is collected in the form of an income tax by the government agencies and later transferred to the respective churches.

In most of the developing countries, religious organizations, particularly stemming from developed states, play an important role in socioeconomic development. In the process of fulfilling their mission of saving lost souls, they are known to provide vital services to their communities, such as building and managing schools and hospitals.   There is therefore a close cooperation between religious bodies and many governments.   In Tanzania, for example, the government provides tax and duty exemptions to religious bodies in support of their

activities in the country.(62)
There is not much on record concerning conflict
arising out of the restriction of the freedom of worship.
The only case which came to our attention of persons being
prosecuted for belonging to an unauthorized religion is
that of R. vs. Elia Abraham and Others.(63) In this case,
the accused persons who professed to a faith known as
"Hema la Sayuni" (The Tent of Zion) were prosecuted for
running an unlawful society, contrary to Section 20 of the
Societies Ordinance. The accused persons had applied for
and refused registration on flimsy political grounds,
particularly since they were being supported by foreign
sources. In the course of the proceedings, it became
clear that the personal beliefs of the individuals were at
issue. The leader of the accused group, Elia Abraham,
claimed that he was a prophet and a descendant of Jesus
Christ, hence leader of Mankind. The accused won the case,
as the state failed to prove its case beyond reasonable
doubt. Nevertheless, the group was denied registration and
hence the right to operate. This was, in a way, a
technical restriction of freedom of worship.(64)
Knowing how sensitive this issue is, the government
has always attempted to handle it with extreme care so as
to avoid chaos. Therefore, there seems to be a cordial
relationship between the government and various religious
organizations. The population is thus allowed to "render
to Caesar what is Caesar's and to God what is God's."
However, since colonial times there have been attempts to
systematically intimidate and suppress certain forms of
religion. These were religions which were seen to be
"anti-development" or generally anti-establishment. These
forms of religions were thus outlawed by the state. They
include the Jehovah's Witnesses or "Watch Tower" Church.
It is alleged that this religion drives its followers into
fanaticism--that they refuse to take modern medicine or go
to hospitals and refuse to sing the national anthem or
salute the national flag. This religion, which has played
a leading role in the struggle against foreign rule and
domination, is still outlawed in Tanzania and affiliation
with it is therefore an offense.(65) There is little, if
any, justification for outlawing religions like the
Jehovah's Witnesses, since that directly conflicts with
the freedom of worship.(66) This freedom is meaningless if
there are boundaries artificially enacted by the state
inhibiting or hindering its total enjoyment.
Again, it is hoped that the Bill of Rights of 1988
will also bring to an end the harassment of small religious
denominations by state agencies. Apart from allowing
splinter denominations within established religions to
register and conduct their activities like everybody else,
it is expected that outlawed religions will also be
decriminalized and rehabilitated and generally allowed to
flourish along with others.

Freedom of Association

Freedom of association entails the right to interact
with other members of the community in any form for the

purposes of pursuing a common interest. It is therefore a
right which enables people to come together without fear of
persecution. The Banjul Charter in Article 10 provides for
the right of every individual to free association which
includes the right not to be compelled to join an
association. The exception to this general rule is found
in Article 29 of the charter. There is a compulsion on the
part of the citizen to join an association for the
purposes of strengthening social and national solidarity
and particularly when national solidarity is being
threatened.

Freedom of association is provided for in the
Tanzanian Bill of Rights, which goes further to guarantee
the right to create or join a party or organization
established with the objectives of maintaining and
promoting faith or interests.(67) The provision on the
freedom of association may turn out to be a source of
problems due to the fact that it directly conflicts with
other parts of the constitution. Article 3 of the
constitution declares Tanzania to be a one-party state and
particularly names Chama Cha Mapinduzi as the sole
political party in the country. This article has to be
read together with Article 10, which says that all
political activities in Tanzania will be carried out either
by the party itself or under its direction or supervision.
The question is whether or not these two provisions are in
conflict with the Bill of Rights and thus invalid.(68)

Addressing the members of the University of Dar es
Salaam Law Society on the Bill of Rights in Tanzania on
September 5, 1985, the Chief Justice of Tanzania, Francis
Nyalali, made reference to this conflict.(69) According to
his Lordship, there is no conflict at all. He argued that
there is a basic structure of the constitution which
establishes, among other things, certain institutions or
organs of state and of the people. Therefore, no provision
of the constitution can be reasonably interpreted or
applied in a manner which effectively abolishes or
diminishes the existence of the role of any such
institution or organ. It therefore logically follows that
the one-party state system, established by Articles 3 and
10 of the constitution, cannot be abolished or diminished
by interpretation of any other provision of the
constitution. Thus, his Lordship concluded that the
freedom of association guaranteed by Article 20(1) does not
include any freedom to form political parties apart from
CCM, which is established by the constitution itself.

The Chief Justice's argument is definitely
interesting, although not very convincing, especially when
one takes into account the fact that Article 20(1)
specifically refers to the right to "establish or join a
Party." Therefore, in our view, the introduction of
differences between political, social, or other types of
"parties" cannot be said to be a convincing interpretation
of the freedom of association as established in absolute
terms in Article 20(1). Maybe it is only practical
experience arising from attempts by individuals to
establish political parties in accordance with the
provisions of the constitution which will shed more light
on the subject. Is the CCM government going to allow

competitors?   It is interesting to note that the chairman
of CCM, Julius Nyerere, who retired   as president of the
United Republic of Tanzania, is reported to have said that
after studying the structure of his party after retiring as
head of state, he has come to the conclusion that there are
flaws in the one-party system.(70)

The over-sensitivity of the party and its government
to any challenge is clearly illustrated by the case of
James Mapalala. Mapalala, on behalf of the Movement for
the Revocation of the One-Party Law, wrote three separate
letters to the chairman and members of the National
Executive Committee of the party, dated August 1, 1985 (in
English), August 7, 1985 (in Kiswahili), and September 28,
1985 (in English). The theme of the three letters was the
same, namely, an appeal for the revocation of the one-party
system in Tanzania and the introduction of a multiparty
system. He did everything openly, without secrecy or
conspiracy. He made it a point to consult experts in
drafting his petition. He consulted Mziray Kangero, an
assistant lecturer in the Political Science and Public
Administration Department of the University of Dar es
Salaam, Professor Sam Ntiro of the Art, Theater and Music
Department of the same university, and Said El Maamry, an
advocate of the High Court of Tanzania and a member of the
Tanganyika Law Society. When the letters reached the
party headquarters in Dodoma, Mapalala and those he
consulted were immediately arrested. They were released
after spending a few days in custody and under heavy
interrogation by the security forces.(71) Mapalala was
subsequently picked up by the police and detained under the
notorious Preventive Detention Act.(72)

The party and the government in Tanzania have
systematically taken away from the people the right to
organize in any form. The two have a monopoly over this
right. Any form of organization has to have a party or
government stamp on it, otherwise it will not be
recognized. This is not accidental. Any ruler knows the
danger of any form of independent organization. It is a
threat to the establishment. Therefore, one should not
wonder that while the freedom of expression can even be
tolerated, the freedom of association has to be issued in
calculated doses. It has been documented that since
independence the government has made it a policy to
infiltrate all forms of mass organization so as to blunt
the sharpness of criticism to the status quo or to derail
these organizations altogether. Where subtle methods have
failed, then force has been used in forms of banning the
organizations or imposing leadership from above.

In other words, there is no way in which the people
can now organize independently of the party. Worse still,
even informal associations in the form of assemblies and
processions in a public place are prohibited in Tanzania.
They may only be organized subject to government permission
issued by the police.(73) The workers' and peasants'
movements have been disbanded and replaced with artificial
organizations which are reduced to organs of the party.(74)
The students have not been left out. Their last
independent movement was banned in 1978 and replaced by a
body which is directly linked to the party's Youth Section.

The history of this systematic muffling of the people's
right to associate and organize has been extensively
analyzed in many works and therefore need not be delved
into further here. One might mention, for example, Issa G.
Shivji's two important books Class Struggles in Tanzania
and Law, State and the Working Class in Tanzania.(75)
      Apart from political restrictions on the freedom of
association which daily loom above the citizen, there are
several technical limitations to the full enjoyment of
this freedom. These are in the form of legislation. The
law in Tanzania makes it extremely hard to form and run an
association. There are various mechanisms available to the
state which enable it to frustrate anybody intending to
realize the freedom of association outside the state-
decreed one-party institutions.
      One of the basic restrictions to this freedom is the
Societies Ordinance, 1954.(76) This law, enacted by the
colonial government and still in force, was mainly aimed at
controlling and monitoring African associations which were
mushrooming in the country, particularly trade unions. It
has been noted that back in the 1940s Africans in various
branches of work had formed associations and unions. These
included the Stevedores and Dockers' Union, the African
Cooks, Washermen and Houseboys' Association, the African
Tailors' Association, and the Dar es Salaam African Motor
Drivers' Union.(77) It was therefore necessary that these
associations and others be carefully monitored so that they
were not a danger to the colonial regime.
      The Societies Ordinance provides for the office of the
Registrar of Societies, who is endowed with wide powers.
The registrar can register or refuse to register any
association. Section 9 of this law says that the registrar
may decline to register any association if:

        he is satisfied that such local society is a
        breach of or is affiliated to or connected with any
        organization or group of a political nature
        established outside Tanganyika....[and if] it appears
        to him that such society is being or is likely to be
        used for any purpose prejudicial to, or incompatible
        with the maintenance of peace, order and good
        Government.(78)

The provision is open and it does not provide any criteria
to guide the registrar in determining whether or not to
register a society. Since the registrar has total
discretion, political influence or pressure is therefore
easily applied.
      The president can also declare any society which is
duly registered unlawful.(79) Once such a declaration has
been made, the condemned society should immediately wind
up its affairs. As a case in point, the president of
Tanzania exercised his powers under the Societies Ordinance
to declare the Ruvuma Development Association to be an
illegal society, simply because there were allegations of
foreign influence in the association coming through
assistance in capital and manpower.(80)
      Furthermore, the Minister for Home Affairs is
empowered by Section 6A of the Societies Ordinance to order

any organization, cooperative, partnership, company, or
association carrying on business activities to register as
a society. This occurs when the minister is of the opinion
that such establishment is carrying on activities other
than business. Once registered under the ordinance, the
establishment falls under the surveillance of the Home
Ministry. The minister is thus empowered to monitor the
activities of all kinds of establishments. This is another
form of limitation of the freedom of association in the
country.

Hand in hand with the restriction of the registration
of associations is the total prohibition of the right to
assemble. Assembling is only one form of realizing the
freedom of association. In an assembly, individuals
associate. The freedom to assemble is restricted purely
because there is a false presumption on the part of the
state that any form of assembly is aimed at either
committing an offense or agitating against the government.
This is clearly seen from the formulation of Section 74 of
the Penal Code:(81)

> When three or more persons assemble with intent
> to commit an offense, being assembled with intent to
> carry out some common purpose, conduct themselves in
> such a manner as to cause persons in neighbourhood
> reasonably to fear that the persons so assembled will
> commit a breach of the peace, or will by such assembly
> needlessly and without any reasonable occasion provoke
> other persons to commit a breach of the peace, they
> are an unlawful assembly.

In a colonial situation such open suspicion of the
indigenous people is understandable. However, it is
surprising that the above section stands unamended today in
the law books.

The Penal Code is complemented by the Police Force
Ordinance;(82) this is another piece of colonial
legislation which prohibits any assembly or procession from
being convened, collected, formed, or organized by any
person except with a valid permit.(83) The ordinance goes
on to authorize any police officer above the rank of
inspector or a magistrate to prevent any such unlawful
assembly from taking place. There is no doubt that the
above laws and many others which hinder the enjoyment of
the freedom of association are aimed at associations which
are of a political nature. These are seen as a threat to
the status quo.

Associations which are nonpolitical are readily
registered by the government. The professional ones among
them are established under statutory provisions. These
include those of Medical Practitioners and Dentists,(84)
Professional Surveyors,(85) and the Tanganyika Law
Society.(86) Though this gives these organizations legal
status, it also gives the state the chance to regulate them
effectively.

Small-scale businesses have also formed associations
in order to protect their own interests. Examples include
the Association of Small Scale Entrepreneurs (1981),
Association of Taxi Drivers (1982), Tanzania Poultry Farmer

Association (1982), Dar es Salaam Transports (Dala Dala)
(1983),   Tanzania   Petrol   Dealers   Association   (1984),
Association of Photographers   (1984),   Tanzania Association
of Parastatal   Organization   (1982),   Food   and   Vegetable
Association (1985), Hotel Keepers   Association (1985),   Fish
&   Fish   Processing   Industries   Association   (1985),   and
Vehicle and Body Builders Association (1985).

As the   names   indicate,   these   are   purely business-
oriented associations   aimed at   building a common front in
bargaining for business rights   and privileges   and against
undue   interference   by   the   party   or government in their
businesses.   Associations   of   this   nature   have   been
encouraged   very   much   of   late   in   the second phase of a
government which is free-enterprise oriented.

Freedom to Participate in National Affairs

Besides being referred to as a   freedom, participation
of the   citizen in   the affairs of his\her nation should be
regarded as a right.   It is one of the pillars of democracy
and was   an antithesis of absolutism during the feudal era.
In the current epoch, the people's demand to participate in
national affairs   is one   of the   forms of struggle against
dictatorship.

The Banjul   Charter provides   for this   right in three
forms.(87)   First, it declares it a right for every citizen
to freely participate in their country's   government either
directly   or   indirectly   through   the   choice   of
representatives. Second, the charter urges equal   access to
public service in the country for all.   The framers of this
document were aware of the emergence   of social   classes in
Africa, which   have vested   interests.   As often happens in
Africa as elsewhere, only a fraction of the   population has
access   to   public   facilities.   These   facilities, which
include public schools, hospitals,   good   roads,   and other
social amenities,   are mainly   centered in   large cities or
towns where   only a   small   percentage   of   the population
lives.   Even   then,   access   to these facilities is often
restricted to the more affluent.   To working-class families
these   facilities   are   physically   near but distant in the
sense of availability.   Third,   the   charter reemphasizes
that the   right of   access to   public property and services
should be on the   basis of   equality.   This   would avoid
creation   of   a   privileged   class having total monopoly of
public amenities which are financed by the taxpayers.

The Bill of Rights of Tanzania, having reiterated what
is   already   elaborated   in   the   Banjul   Charter,   makes a
specific addition.(88)   It   provides   for   the   right and
freedom   of   all   citizens   to   participate   fully   in   the
decisionmaking process on all matters affecting them, their
lives,   or   the nation as a whole.   As usual, this is easier
said than done.   On the surface, it would appear that every
citizen   in   Tanzania   has   the   right   to   participate   in
national affairs. However, reality points to   the opposite.
A clear   example is elections.   Before anyone can stand for
any election, local or national, they have to be cleared by
the   party.   The   party   assumed   the right to choose who
stands and   who   shouldn't,   and   can   reject   an electoral

aspirant without having to justify its decision.
Therefore, for any person aspiring to office in the
country, being in the party's good graces is esssential;
otherwise, there are no real chances.(89)
     There are also constitutional loopholes which make it
possible for very unpopular politicians who cannot face the
electorate to somehow slip into high office without the
people's mandate.(90)   The so-called presidential election
is another indication of the way the population is excluded
from decisionmaking.   Presidential candidates are nominated
by the party and stand alone, without an opponent.   The
electorate has no real choice.(91)   Once candidates get the
required mandate--however marginal--they step into the
highest office in the land.(92)   To call such a process an
election is to distance the term from recognition.   The
choice between two or more candidates is not possible in
Tanzania.
     One positive aspect in the so-called electoral process
in Tanzania is the fact that there is no discrimination
with regard to sex.   Both men and women who have attained
the age of majority (eighteen) have the same right to
participate in the electoral process.   This is positive
compared to what is still taking place in older
democracies.   In Switzerland, for example, women were
barred from participating in federal elections until 1971,
when the law was amended.(93)   In local elections in
Switzerland, women still cannot vote in the canton of
Apenzell, where elections are regarded as men's affairs
from which women should be kept out.(94)
     For the right of citizens to participate in national
affairs to be fully developed there is a need to loosen the
party's grip over all institutions, a situation which has
heretofore stifled democracy.   The rule that everything
should be done under the auspices of the party should be
removed because it severely restricts the parameters of
democratic participation, an act which is in itself
undemocratic. Democracy has to be whole, that is, from the
local up to the national level, without manipulation which
undermines realization of democracy.

          Right to Work and Right to Equal Pay

     The right to work and the right to receive equal pay
for equal work has a long history. It is associated with
the development of the consciousness of the working class
and its organization into trade unions.   The fact that
this right has now been codified, not only in national but
in international legal instruments, is an important step in
the struggle of the workers against exploitation and a
concession on the part of employers.   However, full
realization of this right remains to be achieved and
therefore the struggle must continue.
     The Banjul Charter is unfortunately very brief on this
important right. It simply provides, in Article 15, that
every individual shall have the right to work under
equitable and satisfactory conditions and to receive equal
pay for equal work.   The additional explanation that the
worker is to work under satisfactory conditions should be

taken seriously.   It is aimed   at protecting the worker's
health against all sorts of dangers to life and limb.
      The Bill of Rights separates the   right to   work from
the   right   to fair pay and assigns each a separate
article.(95)   Both   are   thus   guaranteed   under   the
constitution.   This is a surprising turnaround in the
attitude of the leadership toward the rights of workers.
Since independence, there have been systematic, if not
calculated, attempts to deny the right to work.   As Mihyo
observes,

> In Tanzania like in any other capitalist country,
> the   right   to   work is not only unknown   to   the
> Constitution but also to the leaders...The laws that
> have been enacted either   before or after flag
> independence are all out to remove this right. The
> so-called Security   of Employment   Act gives the
> employer a right to dismiss the employee without
> notice. The dispute arising from the dismissal is
> rightly barred from the reactionary courts but pushed
> into tripartite Conciliatory Board which the employer
> combining efforts with the State, his staunch
> supporter, appears again through his representatives
> to pass a binding sentence on the employee, thus
> adding the last nail into his coffin.(96)

      This observation accurately depicts the plight of the
employee.   The so-called Security of Employment Act,
Chapter 574 of the Laws of Tanzania, actually creates
insecurity for the employee.   Apart from providing a
thorough-going disciplinary code and various penalties to
mete out to the worker, it bars labor matters from the open
courts of the law.
      There is a dubious procedure to be followed in
resolving a labor dispute.   In order to maintain so-called
industrial harmony, disputes are resolved in camera and
advocates are not allowed to participate.   There is
therefore no way in which a labor dispute can reach a court
of law   except where an issue of interpretation arises or
where the proceedings of the conciliation board are
conducted in such a manner as to defeat the rules of
natural justice. Even then, the court involved has to
restrict itself to the technicalities.   It cannot address
itself to the merits of the case.(97)
      An interesting addition in the Bill of Rights is on
nondiscrimination--guaranteeing the   right to work and
ensuring that there is equal pay for equal work to all. A
casual look at the employment scene in Tanzania indicates
fairness and lack of discrimination.(98) Where a man and
a woman have the same qualifications and experience for the
same job, the unquestionable practice is that they get
equal pay.   Discrimination on emolument does not exist
either in theory or in practice.(99)
      Again, this is different from the practice in many
developed and industrialized states.   In the Federal
Republic of Germany, for example, one may not be surprised
to find a man being paid more than a woman for the same
type of job.(100)
      The concept of equal pay for equal work should be

given a broader meaning. It should also mean providing workers with wages that will sustain their families rather than merely being what the employer may deem enough. In Tanzania there is a minimum wage (Kima Cha Chini--KCC). However, the sum, which at present stands at Shillings 1260.00 a month (about US$14), is quite unrealistic.(101) It takes the most frugal person less than a week to spend that amount of money. The rest of the month, workers have to look for ways to survive. They usually engage in what is referred to as "Miradi na Mipango"--small projects and side occupations aside from the normal job. Notwithstanding the meagerness of the so-called minimum wage, the government still proudly trumpets any slight additions. The additional amount will be given names--like "Asante Nyerere" ("Thank you, Nyerere"). This is an indication of lack of seriousness on the part of the government in legislating right to work and fair pay when the same government is quite aware that it is not prepared to uphold this right.

The right to work should include the right of the worker to strike. Striking has been one of the ways the working class could enforce its demands for better pay and working conditions, especially where negotiations failed. The fact that workers are in a position to withhold their labor power is a sufficient threat to the employer. In most of the developed and industrialized states, where the labor force is large and powerful, such a right is provided for and guaranteed.

The situation in Tanzania is different. The Permanent Labour Tribunal Act, 1967, came as a serious blow to the workers.(102) First, it removed the basis of a strike, that is, the demand for higher pay and better working conditions. Under this act, the "Trade Union"--which is actually a party organ and has little to do with workers-- is supposed to negotiate with the employer and then register the wage agreement with the Permanent Labour Tribunal. All nonregistered wage agreements have no legal status. The very introduction of registration of wage agreements was intended to control the rise in wages generally. Second, the Permanent Labour Tribunal Act creates a series of conditions which are to be fulfilled before a strike can be called. These conditions make strikes in effect illegal. This shrewd system of offering something in theory and restricting its realization is not limited to Tanzania. Keba M'Baye and Birame Ndiaye note the same with respect to other African countries: "The right to strike is generally recognized, but is regulated in such a way that it scarcely exists, given that in most countries the exercise of that right is subject to government authorities not adopting a solution of conciliation in regard to collective disputes."(103)

That being the case, workers usually decide to strike outside the legal purview. This has taken place on many occasions in Tanzania. Most strikes took place in the 1971-73 period following the party's announcement of the Mwongozo--a policy document which partly touched on the need for respect of workers by managers and bureaucrats.

In the wake of the strikes, the government acted ruthlessly even where clear cases had been made. For instance, when the workers at the Sungura Textile Company laid down their tools in protest against lack of respect for the country's political party and president by the personnel manager, the government closed its ears to the insults. Its statement indicates its docility: "TANU (the then-ruling party) and the Government deplores wild-cat strikes and indiscriminate downing of tools by workers without exhausting the machinery for settling the labour disputes laid down by law. Stern measures would henceforth be taken against any worker or group of workers who would violate the regulations for settling labour disputes as provided by the law."(104)

The government kept its word. The following year the police were deployed against workers in Mount Carmel Rubber Factory. On June 20, 1973, about 69 workers of the factory were arrested, fingerprinted, and repatriated to their home districts. Their crime was that they had rebelled and taken over a factory belonging to an absentee owner who was living abroad but earning his living through the sweat of the Tanzanian workers.(105)

This incident took place on July 27, 1986. The source of the problem was bonus pay for the sugarcane cutters. The management had cut out from the monthly pay of the workers the bonuses which were usually paid to compensate their very low wages of about Shillings 600.00 (about US$6.50) per month. The workers went to the factory gates to demand their bonuses. They peacefully stayed there for the whole day. In the evening the factory management called the Field Force Unit (FFU) from the nearby town of Morogoro. Under the command of the Regional Crimes Officer, Hamidu Mbwezeleni, the force opened fire on the workers, killing three in cold blood.(106)

The killings sparked a flame of angry reactions from people in all walks of life who demanded that those responsible be prosecuted. The government admitted responsibility for the incident and set up a commission of inquiry to conduct investigations.(107) At the same time, the Regional Crimes Officer was removed from his post, pending investigation. As a result of the inquiry, the government in 1987 restructured the management of the Kilombero Sugar Company, sacking and/or transferring various officers.(108) Also affected were the Morogoro Regional Commissioner Crisant Mzindakaya, who was transferred to Kigoma Region, and the Regional Police Commander, Faido Kasongwe, who has been recalled to police headquarters in Dar es Salaam.

Summarizing the performance of his government after one year in office before the party's National Executive Committee in Dar es Salaam on November 30, 1986, President Ali Hassan Mwinyi admitted that the Kilombero killings were a black spot in the history of Tanzania which has tarnished the name of the country within and abroad. He promised to take appropriate steps and to see to it that such a shameful incident will never occur again.(109)

In conclusion, the right to work has to be viewed in totality. The workers should be guaranteed the right to decide on all matters that affect their welfare. This includes the right to strike and to organize in free and genuine trade unions. Creation of bogus and artificial

bodies and designating them as trade unions for the
purposes of deceiving the International Labour Organization
(ILO) and the international community is one form of self-
deceit on the part of those in power. It is also a slap in
the face of this basic human right--the right to work.

Right to Own Property

One of the most cherished rights under capitalism is
the right to private property. Historically, in the
struggle against feudalism the triple demands of the
bourgeoisie equated property with liberty and life itself,
as if no life or liberty were conceivable without property.
Article 14 of the Banjul Charter urges guarantees of
the right to own property. This right should only be
encroached upon in the public interest or in the general
interest of the community--but nevertheless according to
law. The article is general but short. This is quite
understandable coming from a body composed of states with
different attitudes toward property. The article is
actually smoother in language in comparison to Article 17
of the Universal Declaration of Human Rights, which treats
the same theme.
The Bill of Rights of Tanzania is more specific. It
makes reference to the right to own property and for
conditions under which this right can be interfered with.
(110) In the case of nationalization, for instance, the
authorities have to make recourse to the law providing for
procedure for fair compensation.(111) The law referred to
here must be the Foreign Investments (Protection) Act,
1963, which provides for full and fair compensation in case
an approved foreign investment is nationalized,
expropriated, or otherwise compulsorily acquired by the
government.(112)
There were a series of nationalizations in 1967
following the Arusha Declaration, which was a blueprint
for socialism in the country. The aim was to place all
the major means of production under the state. There were
agreements on the amount of compensation to the private
investments affected in this exercise.(113) The problem
is that this act refers to foreign investments only and
not to local investments. However, in 1967 both
foreigners and citizens whose property was nationalized
were equally paid.(114) The enactment of the Bill of
Rights in a way clears the doubt that has been prevailing
for a long time over the safety of private property.
There were substantial fears that the government may, at
any time, grab the individual's property with impunity.
At the same time, the provisions in the Bill of Rights
on the right to ownership of private property are a
departure from a well-known trend that has existed since
independence. This is the trend toward emphasis on
collective right to property as opposed to individual
right. This trend has its basis in traditional African
customs which emphasize the paramountcy of society over the
individual. Though in most African societies the
individual could and did own private property, the
emphasis was on collective ownership.

At the international level, individualism in ownership
of private property has been seriously dented with the
birth of socialism, particularly after the Russian
Revolution. Emphasis has generally shifted toward
collective ownership of property. This new trend is not
restricted to the socialist countries. In the United
Nations, the majority thinking has been toward the concept
of collective ownership. One need only look at UN General
Assembly resolutions on such topics as the right to self-
determination, permanent sovereignty over natural
resources, and the New International Economic Order.(115)
    In most of the developing countries, if not all, the
direct contribution of the right to own private property to
the welfare of the majority has been insignificant because
the majority of the people are dispossessed to begin with,
although it does raise illusions which can rarely be
realized. Such a right is useful only to the wealthy
minority and foreign investors who have or would like to
invest their capital there. This is precisely because this
right will guarantee existing property and is averse to
radical redistribution.

LIMITATIONS TO RIGHTS AND FREEDOMS

Apart from the general limitations which arise out of
the duties and obligations of the individual imposed by
both the Banjul Charter and the Tanzanian Bill of Rights,
which we will discuss later, there exist other forms of
limitations to the rights and freedoms of the individual.
    In the Banjul Charter, the limitations are to be found
in the very articles providing the rights. The normal
phrase used to limit a right or freedom is the added
proviso that such right or freedom is "subject to the
existing law." There are situations, therefore, where a
right is given in the main part of the article and taken
away by the proviso. An example of this is Article 6 of
the Banjul Charter. This controversial article provides in
part that "no one may be deprived of his freedom except
for reasons and conditions previously laid down by law."
This provision may be interpreted to allow deprivation of
freedom where there are laws allowing it, like preventive
detention legislation. This may not be a contravention of
the charter. Although jurists may argue that this is a
simplistic interpretation of the said article, there is no
doubt that such a formulation leaves a lot to be desired.
It ends up sanctioning what it set out to forbid.
    The Tanzanian Bill of Rights has a double limitation.
That is, it provides limitation on the rights and freedoms
of the individual within specific articles and in a special
article meant only for limitation of these rights and
freedoms.(116) Mbunda, in a paper on the limitation
clauses in the Bill of Rights presented at a seminar
marking the silver jubilee of the Dar es Salaam Law School
in 1986, identifies about nine limitation clauses in the
Tanzanian Bill of Rights. These are in Articles 14; 15(2);
16(2); 18(1); 20(1); 20(2); 24(2); and 30(1). The wordings
include such phrases as "in accordance with the law, save
as may be authorized by law," and "subject to any law for

the time being in force."(117)   Therefore, apart from
repeating the well-known maxim that rights have to be
enjoyed or exercised with due care, not to interfere with
or curtail the rights and freedoms of others, the Bill of
Rights empowers the state to enact laws to actualize the
orderly exercise of rights and freedoms.(118)

Declaration of State of Emergency

A declaration of a state of emergency by the state
automatically suspends the exercise of rights and freedoms
as enacted by the Bill of Rights of Tanzania. Article
31(1) provides that the parliament may enact laws allowing
action to be taken during either an emergency or in
peacetime against people believed to be engaged in actions
which endanger or harm the security of the nation.(119)
These are persons deemed to be conducting themselves in a
manner that is dangerous to life contrary to Articles 14
and 15 of the constitution.

This period characterized as an emergency has to be
declared by the president in accordance with the provisions
of Article 32 of the constitution, which empowers the
president to do so. There are situations which might
warrant declaration of a state of emergency:

when the country is in a state of war
when the country is about to be invaded
when there is a threat to national peace or lack of
    security for the people
when there is a definite danger that may lead to
    disruption of peace and public safety
when there is a pending danger or national disaster
    that threatens the society or part of it
when there are other dangers that are obviously a
    threat to the country

When any one or several of the above envisaged situations
occur, a state of emergency may be declared in accordance
with the procedure provided for in the constitution. The
procedure begins with the president declaring the state of
emergency. The president then delivers a copy of the
declaration to the secretary-general of the party and the
speaker of the National Assembly. The two will call a
joint meeting of the party's National Executive Committee
and the National Assembly to deliberate on the declaration.
This has to be done within fourteen days. This joint
meeting is supposed to approve or reject the declaration
made by the president. The declaration has to be approved
by a least two-thirds of the joint meeting, otherwise it
will cease. If approved, the state of emergency will have
to remain in force for six months, if not abrogated before.
It will also cease if not renewed again by the joint
meeting referred to above, which can also by a two-thirds
vote nullify it at any time. Such an elaborate system,
though long and tiresome, is healthy because it checks
arbitrary declaration of a state of emergency, which
entails serious violations of individuals' rights and
freedoms.

OBLIGATIONS AND DUTIES

Human rights in general and fundamental rights in particular are to be seen as a two-way system. There cannot be only rights. There must be duties as well. The connection between rights and duties is a result of the fact that people do not exist in isolation but are social beings. We thus owe certain obligations to others and in the exercise of our rights must take into consideration the rights of others. Also, there are certain forms of rights which can only be enjoyed or exercised collectively. In order to benefit from such rights, individuals must identify themselves with society. This entails, among other things, surrendering certain rights and assuming duties toward society.

Obligations of the Individual under the Banjul Charter

The Banjul Charter provides for duties of the individual in Chapter 2 of Part One, which is composed of Articles 27, 28, and 29. The duties are owed the family, the government, and the community at large. Last, every African has a duty to preserve and promote African unity.(120)

Obligations of the Individual under the Tanzanian Bill of Rights

Unlike the Banjul charter, which is general on the obligations of the individual, the Tanzanian Bill of Rights is specific. It makes reference to four types of obligations: the obligations to work, obey the laws of the country, protect public property, and preserve and maintain national security.(121)

The obligation to work is based on the view of labor alone as a source of social wealth and property in the community and a barometer of humanhood. It is therefore seen as necessary that everybody engage willingly and honestly in legal, productive labor and endeavor to meet the production targets at a personal and collective level. However, the Bill of Rights clearly states that there will be no forced labor.(122) There are situations in which the individual may be forced to work without consent and without this being categorized as forced labor. These include work: as a result of court judgment (prison labor, for instance), in the military as part of the responsibility of serving in the armed forces (including of course the National Service and People's Militia, as a result of an emergency situation (for example, when there is an attack on the country), and as part of relief work to the community (this includes also where there is a natural catastrophe).(123) One cannot rule out the possibility of such exceptions to the general rule against forced labor being used to sanction forced labor and restricting the general freedom of employment.(124)

The obligation to obey the law is straightforward. Article 26 simply imposes the duty on everyone to obey the

constitution and the laws of the United Republic. The
question which has on many occasions occupied legal
philosophers and which we cannot go into at length here, is
whether citizens have a duty to obey oppressive laws, some
of which are retroactive, especially when they are
afforded no opportunity to contribute directly or
indirectly to their formulation. One answer is that the
state can impose the duty on the citizen to obey laws only
where an opportunity is afforded to the citizen to
contribute to the input or revision of such laws. Laws
imposed from above have no justification to claim
respect.(125)

   The duty to protect public property is quite timely.
In the last few years there has been gross disrespect for
public property in Tanzania. This tendency is generally
related to the erosion of patriotism and the development of
strong individualism. The state is no longer seen as a
source of permanent security to the livelihood of the
individual and hence everybody seems to be in a hurry to
take away as much public wealth as the situation allows.
Personal appropriation of community wealth takes two
forms--illegal and "legal." First, there is general
irresponsibility on the part of those entrusted with the
duty of controlling public property and especially
finances. Therefore, every day one reads in the papers of
losses in terms of millions of shillings due to negligence,
theft, or misappropriation. Hundreds of cases of crimes
related to losses in public institutions are still pending
in the courts.(126)

   Second, the so-called "legal" way of taking public
property relates to plunder which is sanctioned by the
state itself through allotment of unjustifiable privileges
to certain sections of the population. The public loses by
way of excessive privileges which bureaucrats in the
government, the party, or other public institutions
immorally assign themselves. For example, a head of a
public institution will assign himself four cars--one for
himself, another for his wife, the third to take the
children to school, and the fourth to service his shamba
(farm) and other small projects. All of these vehicles are
maintained by the taxpayer and instead of offering useful
service to the public, are assigned to one person, whose
contribution to the community is sometimes questionable.
This is only one example of the way the privileged few in
our society cause immeasurable losses to public property.
Therefore, the duty to protect public property in the Bill
of Rights might assist in checking some of these excesses.
Partly for these reasons, President Ali Hassan Mwinyi has
declared war on irresponsibility. It is the hope of the
public that, unlike his predecessors, he will be
thoroughgoing and consistent in his pursuit of reform.(127)

   Article 28 is addressed to all citizens and reminds
them of their patriotic duty to protect, preserve, and
maintain freedom, authority, law, and national unity. To
this end the parliament may enact laws directing people to
join the armed forces in defense of the country. At the
same time, in the case of attack, the people have to fight
for the United Republic to the very end. No one is
allowed to sign an agreement accepting defeat in a war and

to surrender the nation to the victor or to acquiesce or recognize an act of invasion or division of the United Republic or any part of the nation. This article is a direct result of two unrelated experiences. The first was the war between Tanzania and Uganda following the invasion and annexation of the Kagera Salient by Ugandan forces led by the former military dictator Field Marshall Idi Amin Dada.(128)   This was the first postindependence war experience and successful defense of the territorial integrity of the country. The second was the so-called pollution of the political climate in the country in 1983 which led to the stepping down of the second president of Zanzibar, Sheikh Aboud Jumbe Mwinyi. There were allegations that there were moves to remove Zanzibar from the Union.(129)   These might have contributed to the underlining of the need to preserve national unity.

NOTES

    1. See the 1st Article of the Universal Declaration of Human Rights, 1948.   The Declaration is reproduced in United Nations. Yearbook on Human Rights for 1948 (New York: Klaus Reprint Co., 1973), pp. 466-68.

    2. Article 12(1).   This article has to be read together with the general conditions provided in Articles 29(3) and 29(4), which forbid conferring of rights, title, or special honor to any person on the basis of lineage, origin, or inheritance. These two sub-articles were aimed at combatting feudal privileges that go with chieftainship.
    3. See Articles 3 and 7 of the African Charter on Human and People's Rights, and Article 13 of the Tanzanian Constitution.
    4. Article 13(4) of the Constitution of Tanzania, 1977.
    5. Article 13(6)(b).
    6. This principle was discussed in Leeson vs. General Council of Medical Education and Registration (1980) 43 Chancery Division 366.   See also D. C. M. Yardley, Principles of Administrative Law (London: Butterworths, 1981), p. 87.
    7. Article 13(6)(c).
    8. See Amnesty International, Jahresbericht 1977 (Baden-Baden: Nomos Verlagsgesellschaft, 1978), pp. 138-40.
    9. See Amnesty International, Jahresbericht 1977, p. 159.   For the report of the trial of the torturers, see also Amnesty International, Jahresbericht 1979 (Frankfurt: Fischer Taschenbuch Verlag, 1980), pp. 62-63.
    10. See the Review of the International Commission of Jurists, no. 18, June 1977, p. 13.   See also Amnesty International, Jaresbericht 1977, pp. 138-39.   See also "Tanzania: Ministers Resign," Weekly Review (Nairobi), January 31, 1977.
    11. Review of the International Commission of Jurists, p. 13.
    12. See Amnesty International, Jahresbericht 1982 (Frankfurt: Fischer Taschenbuch Verlag, 1982), pp. 114-15.

13. Article 13(b)(c).

14. This principle of law has been discussed at length in various authorities, including the House of Lords' decision in Shaw vs. Director of Public Prosecutions (1962) A.C.220.

15. See Legal Aid Committee (Faculty of Law, University of Dar es Salaam), Essay on Law and Society (Kampala: Sapoba Bookshop Press, 1985), p. 28.

16. See Articles 4, 5, and 6 of the African Charter on Human and People's Rights and Articles 14, 15, and 16 of the Tanzanian Constitution.

17. This point is elaborated in Keba M'Baye and Birame Ndiaye, "The Organization of African Unity (OAU)," in Karel Vasak (ed.), The International Dimensions of Human Rights, Volume 2 (Westport, Connecticut: Greenwood Press, 1982), pp. 583-89.

18. High Court of Tanzania at Arusha, Miscellaneous Criminal Cause No. 22 of (1979). This case is reported in (1981) Tanzanian Law Reports.

19. See, for instance, the case of Happy George Washington Maeda vs. Regional Prisons Officers, Arusha (High Court of Tanzania at Arusha, Miscellaneous Criminal Cause No. 29 of 1979) where the accused was rearrested outside a judge's chambers by security officers after being declared a free person.

20. See Article 14 of the Universal Declaration of Human Rights and Article 12(3) of the African Charter on Human and People's Rights.

21. The episode is narrated in Cranford Pratt, The Critical Phase in Tanzania 1945-1968; Nyerere and the Emergence of a Socialist Strategy (Cambridge: Cambridge University Press, 1976), p. 186.

22. Hatty McGhee escaped from the Keko Remand Prison in Dar es Salaam together with Pius Mutakubwa Lugangira (Uncle Tom). For the trial of those alleged to have facilitated the escape see "Witness Unaware of Prisoners Exchange," Daily News (Tanzania), March 19, 1987.

23. See Amnesty International, Jahresbericht 1984 (Frankfurt: Fischer Taschenbuch Verlag, 1984), pp. 136-39.

24. See H. V. Hodson (ed.), The Annual Register: A Record of World Events 1985, Volume 227 (London: Longman, 1986), p. 220.

25. See H. V. Hodson (ed.), The Annual Register: A Record of World Events 1983, Volume 225 (London: Longman, 1984), p. 214.

26. Article 12(1) and 12(2).

27. Chapter 20 of the Laws of Tanzania.

28. See, for instance, Britain's Detention of Terrorists Order, 1972, discussed at length in Elmar Rauch, "The Compatibility of the Detention of Terrorists Order (Northern Ireland) with European Convention for the Protection of Human Rights," New York University Journal of International Law and Politics 6, no. 1 (1973), p. 1.

29. Part of this legislation is reproduced in Thomas M. Franck, Human Rights in Third World Perspective, Volume 2 (New York: Oceana, 1982), pp. 242-44.

30. See J. K. Nyerere, Freedom and Unity (Dar es Salaam: Oxford UIniversity Press, 1967), p. 305.

31. The most recent detentions under this law are those of James Mapalala and Mwinyijuma Athumani Upindo which were challenged in the High Court. See "High Court Wants Detention Orders," _Daily News_ (Tanzania), November 8, 1986, and "Detention Orders," _Daily News_ (Tanzania), November 11, 1986. Also see, _Index on Censorship_ 16, no. 3 (March 1987), p. 40.

32. See Legal Aid Committee (Faculty of Law, University of Dar es Salaam), _Essays on Law and Society_, p. 35.

33. Chapter 38 of the Laws of Tanzania.

34. See Pratt, _The Critical Phase in Tanzania 1945-68: Nyerere and the Emergence of a Socialist Strategy_, p. 178. See also Ivision Macadam (ed.), _The Annual Register of World Events: A Review of Year 1963_, volume 205 (London: Longmans, 1964), p. 11.

35. High Court of Tanzania at Dar es Salaam, Miscellaneous Criminal Cause No. 21 of 1983 (Unreported).

36. Chapter 39 of the Revised Laws of Tanzania.

37. Act Number 8 of 1969.

38. Act Number 6 of 1983.

39. Act Number 13 of 1973.

40. Chapter 401 of the Revised Laws of Tanzania.

41. Chapter 18 of the Laws of Tanzania.

42. Section 8.

43. See _Daily News_ (Tanzania), April 3, 1973, quoted in David V. Williams, "Law and Socialist Rural Development," _Eastern Africa Law Review_ 6, no. 3 (1973), pp. 193-96.

44. Act Number 11 of 1986.

45. See "Bunge Passes Identity Bill," _Daily News_ (Tanzania), October 25, 1986.

46. See Michael K. B. Wambali, "Freedom of Movement in Tanzania" (mimeo.), a paper presented at a seminar held to commemorate 25 years of the Faculty of Law of the University of Dar es Salaam in October 1986.

47. Article 18.

48. J. K. Nyerere, _Freedom and Socialism_ (Dar es Salaam: Oxford University Press, 1968), pp. 139-41.

49. Information is not a Union matter and hence is handled separately. See Martin Bailey, _The Union of Tanganyika and Zanzibar: A Study in Political Integration_ (Syracuse, N.Y.: Syracuse University Press, 1973).

50. See the Tanzania News Agency Act, 1976 (Act No. 14 of 1976).

51. See "Licensing of Journalists in Tanzania," _Index on Censorship_ 15, no. 6 (June 1986), p. 4.

52. See "Press Censorship under Attack," _Daily News_ (Tanzania), October 25, 1986.

53. See Hadji Konde, _Press Freedom in Tanzania_ (Arusha: Eastern Africa Publications, 1984).

54. Ibid, particularly Chapter 16, titled "Trouble for Newsmen."

55. For a complaint against this crude method used by the government, see "Give the Masses a Chance," _Sunday News_ (Tanzania), August 31, 1986.

56. See Legal Aid Committee (Faculty of Law, University of Dar es Salaam), _Essays on Law and Society_, p. 5.

57. About 85 percent of the population in Tanzania can read and write. This is a credit to the government. It is a big achievement when one compares this with the situation in some developed countries in the West where the level of illiteracy is surprisingly high. In the United States, for example, more than 60 million adults are functional illiterates. This is more than 25 percent of the population. See "Educating America," The Economist (London), May 16, 1987, p. 102. For United States population and other important data, see Andrew Hacker (ed.) U.S.: A Statistical Portrait of the American People (New York: Viking, 1983).

58. Article 8.

59. Article 19(1).

60. Article 19(2).

61. See Articles 4 and 140 of the Constitution of the Federal Republic of Germany. For more explanation, see Erik Wolf, Ordnung der Kirche: Lehr- und Handbuch des Kirchenrechts auf ökumenischer Basis (Frankfurt: Vittorio Kostermann, 1961), p. 142, where he discusses "guarantee of the tax base."

62. See United Nations, Yearbook on Human Rights for 1977-1978 (New York: UN Secretariat, 1982), p. 165.

63. (1977) Resident Magistrates Court, Moshi (Unreported).

64. This case was brought to our attention by Mr. Alex T. Nguluma of the Faculty of Law, University of Dar es Salaam, who participated in the proceedings. He discusses it in his paper "The Right of Association in Tanzania: Its Origins and Development" (mimeo.), Faculty of Law, University of Dar es Salaam, 1986.

65. See Marie-Louise Martin, Kimbangu: An African Prophet and His Church, translated by D. M. Moore (Oxford: Basil Blackwell, 1975) and Werner Ustorf, Afrikanische Initiative: Das aktive Leiden des Propheten Simon Kimbangu (Bern: Herbert Lang, 1975), for the experience in Zaire.

66. For an interesting legal discussion on the right to profess religious beliefs and disbeliefs, see the Zambian case of Feliya Kachasu (an infant by her father and next friend Paul Kachasu) vs. Attorney-General, High Court of Zambia at Lusaka, Civil Jurisdiction Selected Judgments of Zambia, No. 10 of 1969 (1967/HP/273). This case is reproduced in Thomas M. Franck, Human Rights in Third World Perspective, Volume 3 (New York: Oceana, 1982), p. 325.

67. Article 20.

68. Normally, any article of the constitution or any law which is in conflict with the provisions of the Bill of Rights is invalid. An example is provided in the Canadian Case of R. vs. Drybones (1970) S.C.R. 282, also reproduced in John D. Whyte and William R. Ledermann, Canadian Constitutional Law (Toronto: Butterworths, 1977). In this case, a law which was discriminatory to the Canadian Indians was declared invalid by the Canadian Supreme Court. Also, see the Sudanese case of J. A. Garang and Others vs. the Supreme Commission of Sudan and Others, 1968, Sudan Law Reports. In this case, the Sudanese government sought to bar Communist activities.

69. See Francis Nyalali, "The Bill of Rights in Tanzania," a public lecture delivered on September 5, 1985 at the Faculty of Law, University of Dar es Salaam (unpublished).

70. See African Research Bulletin, July 15, 1986, pp. 813-14.

71. See S. E. A. Myungi, "Impact of Party Supremacy Doctrine on Democratic Process of Government in Tanzania" (mimeo.), Master of Laws Dissertation, University of Dar es Salaam, 1986.

72. See Index on Censorship 16, no. 3 (March) 1987, p. 40.

73. This requirement is indicated in section 40 of the Police Force Ordinance, Chapter 322 of the Laws of Tanzania.

74. Workers' and peasants' organizations are now established under Article 80 of the Constitution of the Chama Cha Mapinduzi (CCM). The same is the case for the United Women's Organization (UWT). In these cases the organizations become organizations of and not for the persons they are meant for. This observation is also made in the context of the women's organizations elsewhere. See, for instance, Margaret Strobel, "From Lelemama to Lobbying: Women's Associations in Mombasa, Kenya," in Nancy J. Hafkin and Edina G. Bay (eds.), Women in Africa.

75. See Issa G. Shivji, Class Struggles in Tanzania (London: Heinemann, 1976) and Law, State and the Working Class in Tanzania (London: James Currey, 1986). Also relevant are the following works: Isa G. Shivji (ed.), The State and the Working People in Tanzania (Dakar: Codesria, 1985); Henry Mapolu and Issa G. Shivji, Vuguvugu la Wafamyakazi Nchini Tanzania (Kampala: East Africa URM Contact Group, 1984); David R. Morrison, Education and Politics in Africa: The Tanzanian Case (London: C. Hurse, 1976); and Andrew Coulson, Tanzania: A Political Economy (Oxford: Clarendon, 1982).

76. Chapter 337 of the Revised Laws of Tanzania.

77. See Shivji, Law, State and the Working Class in Tanzania, p. 162.

78. Section 9 has to be read together with Section 12 of the same ordinance.

79. Section 6.

80. See Martin, Personal Freedom and the Law in Tanzania, p. 35. See also Coulson, Tanzania: A Political Economy, p. 319.

81. Chapter 16 of the Revised Laws of Tanzania.

82. Chapter 322 of the Revised Laws of Tanzania.

83. Section 40(8).

84. Act Number 20 of 1979.

85. Chapter 409 of the Laws of Tanzania.

86. Tanganyika Law Society Act, Chapter 334 of the Laws of Tanzania.

87. Article 13.

88. Article 21.

89. A clear case is that of Wolfgang Dourado, a former attorney-general of Zanzibar and a seasoned government critic, whose attempt to enter the Zanzibar House of Representatives during the 1985 elections was aborted by the NEC although he was popular with the electorate, as

indicated in the primaries. On this "foul play" by the
NEC, see Africa Events (London), November 1985, p. 28.
    90. Shivji discusses at length various cases of the
executive bringing back into office unpopular characters
who had been rejected by the people. See Issa G.
Shivji, "The State of the Constitution and the Constitution of the
State in Tanzania," Eastern African Law Review 11-14 (1978-
81), p. 1.
    91. For the election of the president, see Article 38
of the Constitution of Tanzania and also Presidential
Elections Act, 1984 (Act No. 15 of 1985), particularly
Section 9.
    92. For example, in the 1985 general elections in
Tanzania the party's sole presidential candidate for
Zanzibar, Idris Abdul Wakil Nombe, was declared duly
elected after getting only 61.25 percent of the total votes
cast. See Sunday News (Tanzania), October 20, 1985.
    93. See Christoph Winzeler, Die politischen Rechte des
Aktivburgers nach schweizerischem Bundesrecht (Basel:
Helbing & Lichtenhahan, 1983), p. 18. In the United
States, women began voting in 1920, about 133 years after
independence. See "The Long March of the Law," Newsweek
(United States), May 25, 1987, p. 33.
    94. See Part V of the Constitution of Kanton
Appenzell A.Rh. of 1908 and Part V of the Constitution of
Kanton Apenzell I.Rh. of 1872.
    95. See Articles 22 and 23 respectively.
    96. See Paschal Mihyo, "The Struggle for Workers'
Control in Tanzania, Review of African Political Economy
(May-October, 1975), p. 70-71.
    97. See, for instance, Ally Linus and Eleven Others
vs. Tanzania Harbours Authority, High Court of Tanzania at
Dar es Salaam, Miscellaneous Civil Cause No. 5 of 1980, in
which, following an application for certiorari and
mandamus by the workers through the Legal Aid Committee of
the Faculty of Law, University of Dar es Salaam, the High
Court quashed the proceedings before the Labour
Conciliation Board at Temeke, Dar es Salaam. The same
happened in Amri Juma and Fifteen Others vs. Tanzania
Harbours Authority, High Court of Tanzania at Dar es
Salaam, Miscellaneous Civil Cause No. 37 of 1980.
    98. See the Employment Ordinance, Chapter 366 of the
Laws of Tanzania, and Jane Rose K. Kikopa, Law and the
Status of Women in Tanzania (Addis Ababa: African Training
and Research Centre for Women--United Nations Economic
Commission for Africa, 1981), p. 55.
    99. It is hoped that this form of equality will also
be accommodated in other areas so as to ensure total
emancipation of women, which, as the late President Machel
of Mozambique correctly put it, is not a charity but a
right. He is quoted in Leith Mullings, "Women and Economic
Change in Africa," in Nancy J.l Hafkin and Edino G. Bay
(eds.), Women in Africa: Studies in Social and Economic
Change, p. 257.
    100. See Claudia Pinl, "Ursachen der ungleichen
Bezahlung von Männern und Frauen und bisherige Strategien
zu Ihrer Überwindung," in Marielouise Janssen-Jurreit
(ed.), Frauenprogramm gegen Diskriminierung (Hamburg:
Rowohlt Taschenbuch Verlag, 1979); Annemarie Renger,

Gleiche Chancen für Frauen? (Heidelberg: C. F. Muller
Juristischer Verlag, 1977; and Luc Jochimsen, Sozialismus
als Männersachen oder kennen Sie "Bebels Frau?" (Hamburg:
Rowohlt Taschenbuch Verlag, 1978). See also Anna
Dunnebier, "Musterprozess: Gleicher Lohn für gleiche
Arbeit," Emma, August 1978, p. 48.
    101. See "Minimum Wage Now 1260.00," Daily News
(Tanzania), May 2, 1987.
    102. Act No. 41 of 1967.
    103. See M'Baye and Ndiaye, "The Organization of
African Unity (OAU)" in Vasak, The International Dimensions
of Human Rights, p. 598.
    104. See Daily News (Tanzania), August 26, 1972.
    105. Mihyo chronicles the various strikes in the
country in 1971-73 and the way the government handled them.
See Mihyo, "The Struggle for Workers' Control in Tanzania."
    106. The respected London-based journal Africa Events
(volume 2, no. 9, September 1986) treats the Kilombero
killings in four different articles: "Kilombero Killings,"
p. 49; "Glimpses from Labour History," pp. 41-42; "Bitter
Sweetener," p. 42; and "Policing Tanzania: The Role of
FFU," p. 43.
    107. See "Kilombero Management Restructured," Daily
News (Tanzania), January 19, 1987.
    108. See "Kilombero Findings Out Soon," Daily News
(Tanzania) January 19, 1987.
    109. See Hotuba ya Rais Ali Hassan Mwinyi Akizungumza
na Wajumbe wa Halmashouri Kuu ya Taifa ya CCM, Dar es
Salaam Tarehe 30-11-1986 Kuhusu Mwaka Mmoja wa Uongozi
wake. This Swahili speech, which was the report of the
president to the party's National Executive Committee over
his first year in office, was widely circulated; see Daily
News (Tanzania), December 1, 1986.
    110. Article 24(1).
    111. Article 4(2).
    112. Act No. 40 of 1963, which is Chapter 533 of the
Laws of Tanzania.
    113. For an analysis of the 1967 nationalizations see
Clarence Dias, "Tanzanian Nationalizations: 1967-1970,"
Cornell International Law Journal 4, no. 1 (1970), p. 59;
James H. Mittelman, Underdevelopment and Transition to
Socialism: Mozambique and Tanzania (New York: Academic
Press, 1981); Reginald H. Green, "A Guide to Acquisition
and Initial Operation: Reflections from Tanzanian
Experience 1967-1974," in Julio Faundez and Sol Picciotto
(eds.), The Nationalization of Multinationals in
Peripheral Economies (London: Macmillan, 1978); J. K.
Nyerere, "Public Ownership," in Freedom and Socialism (Dar
es Salaam: Oxford University Press, 1968); Dianne Bolton,
Nationalization--A way to Socialism? The Lessons of
Tanzania (London: Zed Books, 1985); and Peter Neerso,
"Tanzania's Policies on Private Foreign Investment," in
Carl Widstrand, Multinational Firms in Africa (Dakar:
African Institute for Economic Development and Planning,
1975).
    114. See Dias, Ibid.
    115. See Declaration on the Granting of Independence
to Colonial Countries and Peoples, UN General Assembly
Resolution 1514 (XV), December 14, 1960; Permanent

Sovereignty over Natural Resources, UN General Assembly Resolution 1893 (XVII) of 1962; and Declaration on the Establishment of the New International Economic Order (NIEO), UN General Assembly Resolution 3201 (S-VI), May 1, 1974.

116. Article 30.

117. See L. X. Mbunda, "Limitation Clauses in the Bill of Rights" (mimeo.), a paper presented at a seminar held to commemorate 25 years of the Faculty of Law of the University of Dar es Salaam in October 1986.

118. Article 30(1) and 30(2).

119. Actually the parliament has already enacted a law to take care of the situation envisaged here. This law, the Emergency Powers Act, 1986 (Act Number 1 of 1986) repeals the Emergency Powers Orders in Council 1939 to 1961. It confers upon the president certain emergency powers for purposes of ensuring safety and maintenance of public order during emergencies.

120. Article 29(8).

121. Articles 25, 26, 27, and 28 respectively.

122. Article 25(2).

123. Article 25(3).

124. The concept of freedom of employment and its application in the African context is discussed by M'Baye and Ndiaye, "The Organization of African Unity (OAU), in Vasak, The International Dimensions of Human Rights, pp. 596-97.

125. On the question of whether citizens have a duty to obey oppressive and at times immoral laws, see the celebrated debate between two eminent jurists in H. L. A. Hart, "Positivism and the Separation of Law and Morals," and Lon L. Fuller, "Positivism and Fidelity to Law--A Reply to Professor Hart," in Harvard Law Review 71, no. 4 (1958), pp. 593, 630.

126. See, for example, "Tanesco Manager in 7.9 Million Shillings Scandal," Sunday News (Tanzania) May 10, 1987; "Six in Court over 4 Million Shillings Coffee Theft," Daily News (Tanzania), March 31, 1987; "Doctor on 3 Million Shillings Theft Charge," Daily News (Tanzania), February 20, 1987; and "Woman Cashier Lands in Jail," Daily News (Tanzania), March 27, 1987.

127. In the process of trying to clean up the dominant bureaucracy and create efficiency, the president has sacked a few top bureaucrats, including the general manager of the Tanzanian Railways Corporation and the director-general of the National Provident Fund (NPF). However, the people are demanding a thorough shake-up. See "Kiltex G. M. Dismissed," Daily News (Tanzania), March 19, 1987; "The President Fires the NPF Director-General," Sunday News (Tanzania), August 3, 1986; and Adam Lusekelo, "The Iron Broom," African Events (London) 2, no. 9 (September 1986).

128. See H. V. Hodson (ed.), The Annual Register: World Events in 1978 (London: Longman, 1979), pp. 212-14; and Mahmood Mamdani, Imperialism and Fascism in Uganda (Nairobi: Heinemann Educational Books, 1983), pp. 107-108.

129. On this whole issue, see Anver Versi, "Zanzibar in Turmoil," New African (London), March 1984, p. 19.

Chapter 3
People's Rights

The peculiar aspect of the African Charter on Human and People's Rights is the inclusion of what are termed people's rights in this document.(1) This indicates a major departure from the traditional format adopted by most international instruments on human rights.(2) The enunciation of the new concept of people's rights, which is missing in all hitherto existing documents, is what makes the African Charter both controversial and interesting.

Human rights, as known today, are a product of capitalist society, which sees the importance of the individual as the center of everything in society. It is therefore not surprising that most fundamental rights and freedoms are aimed at the individual. People's rights, on the other hand, tilt the focus from the individual to the wider society. These are rights which the individual can enjoy as a member of a particular society, together with others. In a way, this is socialization of human rights by taking them back to where the individual belongs--within the society.

The African Charter has been assailed for ambiguity as far as people's rights are concerned.(3) The main concern of most writers and critics is the lack of definition of the term "people's" in the charter. While the rights themselves are rather clear, it is not clear to whom they are supposed to pertain. Who benefits from these rights? Who are the people? Some writers have argued that the term was left hanging in the air in order to avoid controversy within the OAU(4) and in international law, generally.(5)

Whatever may have been the reason for this lacuna, it must be appreciated that the coinage of the term "people's" had two edges. On the one hand, it was to differentiate the individual from society and on the other, it was to mark the border between the state and its citizens. This is because the state does not necessarily represent the views of the majority of its citizens. Occasions can therefore arise whereby people can demand their rights directly from the state itself. There are also rights which a state and its people have against foreign entities. These may be political or economic and the African Charter brings this out in sharp relief.

THE ORIGIN OF PEOPLE'S RIGHTS

It is true that the African Charter was not the first document or forum in which the term "People's" was applied in connection with rights. As Kiwanuka notes, as far back as 1790 the decree of the French Constituent Assembly made reference to both rights of man and rights of peoples.(6) The term has also been used in international circles in connection with the right to self-determination.(7) There is also a close relationship, at least at a conceptual level, between people's rights as formulated in the African Charter and the socialist theory of citizens' rights.(8) This is, however, highly contested by some authors who insist on the uniqueness of the African situation which gives rise to such rights.(9)

It is interesting the way the whole concept of people's rights came to be included in the charter. It was the African countries with leftist leanings which insisted on inclusion of this form of rights. During the OAU summit in Monrovia in 1979, Madagascar and Guinea declared that they would not support the charter if people's rights were not included. It is their stubbornness which led to the historic decision to include these rights in the document.(10)

The question that follows is, what are these rights? The type of rights categorized as people's rights in the charter include the rights to equality; existence, self-determination, free disposal of wealth and natural resources, economic, social, and cultural development, national peace and security, and a satisfactory environment.(11) These are very broad rights and, to some extent, quite distinct from each other.

Conceptually, people's rights have different sources and their time of emergence and the reasons behind them also differ. We proceed to examine what may be taken as sources of some of the people's rights. First, the right to self-determination is closely related to colonialism--a form of domination of one people by another.

Various writers in international law have attempted to define the concept of self-determination. For example, the Brazilian jurist Palmeira says: "Self-determination is the legal formula for a people's political and economic independence. It means that every nation, State, or people has the right to determine its political system, solve its domestic problems as it wishes and freely trade with other States, nations and peoples without any international control."(12)

Another writer, Levin, says that "self-determination is the right of the people of a nation freely, without outside pressure, to determine their affiliation, including the right to form an independent State, and also to determine the forms of their internal political, economic, social, and cultural life which is guaranteed by international organizations and bodies."(13) Some authors add to this definition the controversial right of secession, which is still heatedly debated in international law circles.(14)

The basic characteristics of this concept are given by Professor Umozurike. These are: government according to the will of the people; the absence of internal and external domination; the free pursuit of economic, social, and cultural development; the enjoyment of fundamental human rights and equal treatment; and the absence of discrimination on the grounds of class, caste, creed, or political conviction.(15)

It is said that the concept was first used in domestic politics before it found the present popularity in the international arena at the end of the eighteenth century.(16)   It was concretely entrenched in historic records during the American Revolution of 1776 and the French Revolution of 1789.(17)   Most writers are agreed that it was on these two occasions that the concept received its first practical application.(18)

The charter of the United Nations, in Articles 1 and 55, incorporates it and in so doing makes it an integral part of positive international law. In 1960 the UN General Assembly passed an important resolution as far as this concept is concerned.   This was Resolution 1514 (XV) of December 14, 1960, called the Declaration on the Granting of Independence to Colonial Countries and Peoples. Over time, the concept of self-determination has managed to carve a place for itself among other peremptory norms or rules of jus cogens, such as <u>pacta sunt servanda</u> and <u>clausula sic stantibus</u>.   Therefore, what the African Charter on Human and People's Rights did was underline and reemphasize the importance of this concept, in particular in the African context, bearing in mind the fact that Africa has been and still is one of the greatest victims of colonialism and foreign domination.

Second, the right to freely dispose of wealth and natural resources is also connected with colonialism, in particular economic domination of one nation by another or agencies of another.(19)

The process of colonialism was spearheaded by investors who were searching for raw materials, cheap labor, and markets.   Administrative facilities in the colonies were instituted to ensure that these three main needs of the metropolis were assured.   Little changed at independence of the former colonies. The economies of the newly freed states continued (and still continue) to depend on the directions of the former masters who, together with other developed states, indirectly control them through the mechanism of the now-famous multinational corporations.   The people in the former colonies, notwithstanding their new status, are not masters of their own destiny. The international community needs to ensure that all peoples have total control of their natural resources. The UN has been in the forefront of this process.

The first UN General Assembly resolution on this issue was in 1952. This was Resolution 626 (VII) of December 21, 1952, titled "The Right to Exploit Freely the Natural Wealth and Resources."   It was followed by several other resolutions, some making reference to particular parts of the world where there was clear denial by foreigners to the indigenous people of the right to their resources.

Another general resolution came ten years later.   This was
Resolution 1893   (XVII) of December 14,   1962, called
"Permanent Sovereignty over Natural Resources."(20)   The
resolutions on the New International Economic Order, the
Program of Action on the New International Economic Order
of May 1974,(21) and the Charter of Economic Rights and
Duties of States(22) made extensive reference to the right
of the people to have permanent sovereignty over their
natural resources and wealth.
       Third, the right to development is one of what are
referred to as third-generation human rights.(23) This
right is said to be relatively new(24) although the quest
for development has existed for centuries.(25) The right
to development can easily be related to the right to
permanent sovereignty over natural resources because it is
a realization of the glaring fact that one part of the
globe is highly developed while the other is not.
Therefore, various forums have implicitly been discussing
this right without concretizing it as a right. These
forums range from the United Nations Conference on Trade
and Development (UNCTAD) to many others dealing with the
so-called North-South dialogue.   The formulation of the
plight of the people of the developing countries as a right
was done for the first time by the Algerian Commission on
Justice and Peace in its report titled "The Right of
Underdeveloped Peoples to Development," published in
1969.(26)
       However, the person credited with bringing this right
to the attention of the international community is Justice
Keba M'baye, the current vice-president of the
International Court of Justice (ICJ).   At the invitation of
Rene Cassin, the founder of the International Institute of
Human Rights at Strasbourg, to make an inaugural lecture in
1972, M'baye chose to talk about the right to
development.(27) According to M'baye himself, it was the
first time that anyone had talked about the right to
development.(28) Fortunately, this was at about the same
time that the director of this institute, Karel Vasak,
launched his theory of the evolution of a third generation
of human rights.(29) The two gentlemen became very active
in promoting their new ideas.   They played an important
role in securing the adoption of a resolution by the Human
Rights Commission in 1977 calling for a study on the
international dimension of the right to development.
       A boost to this right came in 1978 when the UN
General Assembly in the "Declaration on the Preparation of
Societies for Life in Peace," stated categorically that
all peoples have the right to determine the road to their
development.(30) The right was formally recognized through
the General Assembly Resolution 34/46 of 1979 which said,
inter alia, that the right to development is a human right
and that equality of opportunity for development is as
much a prerogative of nations as of individuals within
nations.(31) Since then the popularity of this right has
increased and the African Charter became the first legal
document to embody it.(32)
       Fourth, the right to national and international peace
and security found in the charter of the United Nations
itself. The original aim of the formation of the UN, as is

clearly reflected in the charter, was to promote peace and security in the world after the horrors of two world wars.(33) This quest for peace has been echoed in almost all international instruments that have appeared since 1945.(34)

However, although peace and security has been the catch phrase for both politicians and experts, it has never appeared to them that the same should be formulated as a right. It is the African Charter that for the first time proclaims peace as a right.(35)

Fifth, the right to a satisfactory environment is said to be the newest in international human rights circles.(36) It also falls under the third-generation rights. The right to a clean environment is a byproduct of industrialization. However, even in the period before heavy industrial development there had been environment-related initiatives aimed at the protection of nature and some of its objects. These initiatives have focused on the protection of birds(37) and animals,(38) conservation of nature in particular areas,(39) prevention of pollution of rivers,(40) lakes,(41) or marine zones and similar topics.

Serious steps in formulating rules and regulations on environmental protection began before the 1960s and climaxed with the calling of the United Nations Conference on the Human Environment in Stockholm in June 1972.(42) This conference recommended, among other things, the establishment of a Governing Council for the United Nations Environment Program (UNEP). The General Assembly endorsed this recommendation by adopting Resolution 2997 (XXVII) of December 15, 1972, which established the UNEP Governing Council.(43) UNEP is based in Nairobi, Kenya.(44)

The recommendations by the Stockholm conference were based on the fact that humankind is the custodian of the earth and that we have reached a point in history where we must shape our actions with more prudent regard to their environmental consequences. On the duty of states in environmental protection, the conference said that: "States have, in accordance with the Charter of the United Nations and the principles of international law, the sovereign right to exploit their resources pursuant to their own environmental policies, and the responsibility to ensure that activities within their jurisdiction or control do not cause damage to the environment of other States or areas beyond the limits of national jurisdiction."(45)

This principle was later incorporated into various international instruments, including the Charter of Economic Rights and Duties of States of 1981(46) and the United Nations Law of the Sea Convention of 1982.(47)

Recently, a World Commission on Environment and Development established by the United Nations under the chairmanship of the prime minister of Norway, Mrs. Gro Harlem Brundtland, published its report.(48) In this report, the 22 commissioners, drawn from all geographical areas of the globe, urge all the countries of the world to do something for the environment. According to the commissioners, protection of the environment is not only important to us but also "for our children's future."(49)

All these efforts notwithstanding, living in a clean

environment was never considered a right that could be promoted and protected. The suggestion that the scope of what are regarded as human rights should be extended to cover environment was made for the first time in 1974 by Rene Cassin. In his Hague Academy of International Law lecture, the Nobel Peace Prize winner said that "the existing concepts of human rights protection should be extended in order to include the right to a healthful and decent environment, i.e., freedom from pollution and the corresponding rights to pure air and water."(50)

The African Charter was the first international instrument to respond to Cassin's call by proclaiming the right to a satisfactory environment as a human right to which all peoples are entitled.

From the above analysis, it is clear that what are categorized as people's rights are diverse. The demands for these rights arose at different points in time in history. They were demands arising out of concrete material conditions and struggles in the process of the development of society.

However, notwithstanding their different origins, the philosophy behind them in different parts of the world where they are advocated is more or less identical: society transcends the individual. They refer to a sort of common rights which are to be enjoyed by all in the community. They do not, however, in any way involve the subordination of the individual to society or give society preference over and above the individual. Membership in a particular society becomes a condition quo non to the enjoyment of this form of right.(51)

The philosophy behind people's rights as they are set out in the African Charter is one and the same. In the African context, people's rights can be traced to the old African traditions which have always taken the individual as part and parcel of society. Society was, and in most African societies still is, given preference over individuals and their specific and personal needs. This could be said to be the basis of patriotism. That is, the individual was educated to put society first. This is what Senghor had in mind when he reminded the experts preparing the charter to "keep constantly in mind our values of civilization and the real needs of Africa."(52)

The traditions referred to here are those in precolonial society, in which there existed a close and complementary relationship between the individual and society. This system worked very well in the communal way of life which existed in most areas in Africa prior to the coming of colonialism, which completely destroyed this socioeconomic system. The brutal destruction of this way of life may be said to be one of the factors which brings nostalgia to most Africans, including those on the top (and who are the beneficiaries of the current system) and a desire to "go back." It is also a testimony of the refusal to accept that colonialism is a reality which took place and had the effect of implanting foreign production relations accompanied by a new culture at the super-structural level.

Although it is very attractive, the philosophical basis of people's rights remains highly idealistic. It is true that we must learn from the past as that is the only way we can forge ahead. However, we must improve on that. What Babu says in connection with learning about democracy from our past is not irrelevant to our conceptualization of fundamental rights and freedoms as they were practiced in the past in African societies:

> The politics and the ideology of the past were the concentrated expression of their economics, the economics of the past, and have no relevance to the economics of the present or of the future...if these early forms of social organization also contained elements of democracy, it was the democracy of the particular time, totally unfitted to the democratic practice of man in the present epoch. To say that an African can learn democracy simply by looking back to see how our great-grandparents behaved is not only meaningless but downright reactionary.(53)

However, such a common past is an important rallying point for Africans, particularly when articulated by personalities such as Senghor.   This is one of the few things Africans still share--a common past.

CONTENT OF THE PEOPLE'S RIGHTS IN THE AFRICAN CHARTER

The African Charter provides for six types of rights which "all" people are entitled to.   These are the rights to equality,(54) existence and self-determination,(55) free disposal of natural wealth and resources,(56) develop-ment,(57) peace and security,(58)   and a satisfactory environment.(59)   We proceed to elaborate on these rights while emphasizing their importance to the African continent.

Equality of Peoples

Article 19 provides that all people are equal and shall enjoy the same respect and rights. This provision is of extreme value in the African context due to various differences which exist among the African people. These differences are national, regional, subregional, and inter-national within the continent.

Differences among various nationalities (sometimes referred to as tribes) in Africa existed long before colonialism. This was because a particular nationality was effective at war and could fight, defeat, and enslave another. The very act of enslavement created deep tensions among various nationalities. Also, poverty arising out of natural or other forms of catastrophe pushed some nationalities into enslavement by the rich and well-off nationalities. These differences were enhanced during the colonial period, particularly by the Church. Various facilities and "development" or "civilization" projects such as schools and hospitals were offered according to the loyalty of a particular nationality to the colonial masters. This means that the nationalities that refused to compromise their freedom and identity were earmarked as troublesome and denied these facilities when it was not though necessary to fight them to total submission. This had the effect of creating not only differences in advancement but also deep enmity among different peoples. African history is full of loyalists and those who stood their ground and refused to bend. For the latter the price was equally high. It is not therefore surprising that in some countries in Africa the nationalities in the minority are the ones in control of everything because they embraced the colonialists and managed to gain access to modern facilities early. This has created open and serious inequalities among peoples within a state. Clashes among various nationalities in Africa are still prevalent and are fueled by the ruling elite, who gain from the division among the people.(60)

Another source of inequality on the continent is color. Although it is rarely admitted in public, it is true that there are regions in Africa in which the distribution of basic commodities and economic, social, and other facilities among the people is done on the basis of color of the inhabitants. This discrimination on the basis of color has led to civil wars that are in some cases a threat to national unity.(61) There are also confirmed reports of the reemergence of slavery in some African countries based on color. That is, people of one color within a country who are already economically disadvantaged are enslaved by others who feel superior and have the material means of exercising superiority.(62)

Given this problematic set-up, the emphasis on equality of all people cannot be taken lightly in Africa and its inclusion in the charter is more than timely. It is essential that the political, economic, or cultural advantage of one people should not be used as a justification for suppressing or disadvantaging others.

Right to Existence and Self-Determination

The right of all people to existence, self-determination of their political status, and pursuit of the economic and social development of their choice is provided for in Article 20.

The first part of this article is aimed at curbing genocide, which is not foreign to Africa. There are many known cases of genocide on the continent. These range from the German war against the Hereros and Namas in South-West Africa (now Namibia) during the colonial period to the clashes between the Hutus and the Tutsis in Burundi, which keep on happening from time to time. It is also a fact that the source of the Biafran War in Nigeria was genocide. Ibos from the eastern part of the country were being murdered simply because they were Ibos.(63) International law recognizes genocide as one of the crimes against humanity.(64) Therefore the charter underlines this position taken by the international community.

The second part of the article refers to the right of all people to self-determination.(65) It goes on to provide that colonized or oppressed people have the right

to free themselves from the bonds of domination by
resorting to any means recognized by the international
community.

Africa may be the only continent which has suffered
heavily and for a long time from colonial domination. With
the exception of Liberia and Ethiopia, the rest of Africa
was at one point or another under colonial rule. To date,
colonialism and oppression of parts of the continent
continue. This puts the issue of self-determination on
the top of every agenda in any forum in Africa. The right
of self-determination also finds support in other important
international instruments, such as the charter of the
UN.(66) In battling colonialism, the international
community now recognizes the right of colonized people to
resort to all means available to them, including armed
struggle.(67)

The last part of Article 20 urges states signatory to
the charter to assist those struggling for their liberation
against foreign domination. The OAU has been in the forefront in the struggle against colonialism and has established a liberation committee which coordinates assistance
to those fighting for the liberation of their countries.

It is worth noting that while the charter provides
that this assistance should be to combat political,
economic, and cultural domination, in reality the OAU has,
in most cases, restricted itself to political struggles
only. This is not accidental. Any attempt to counter the
other two forms of domination (i.e., economic and cultural)
comes into direct clash with Article 3(2) of the OAU
Charter of 1963, which prohibits states from interfering
with the internal affairs of others.(68)

Right to Free Disposal of Natural Wealth and Resources

The inclusion of the right of each people to freely
dispose of their natural resources and wealth is in a way a
recognition of the principle of permanent sovereignty over
natural resources as developed through the United Nations
and now recognized by the international community as part
of international law.(69) The realization of this right by
the people of Africa is to be through the state. This can
be easily inferred from the very formulation of Article
21(1). This subarticle provides that the right is to be
exercised in the exclusive interest of the people.

The exercise of this right is subject to the
obligations of all states to promote international
cooperation on the basis of mutual respect, equitable
exchange, and the principles of international law. This is
done with clear realization of the known fact that the so-
called world market does not provide fair and equitable
exchange of resources to all. As African and developing
countries in general have justifiably complained over the
years, the market is unequal and tilted in favor of the
developed states. The prices of industrial products of
developed states rise year after year while those of
agricultural products from developing countries remain
stagnant or drop. The reference to equality in exchange is
aimed at counteracting this unhealthy economic tendency.

Reference to principles of international law in
connection with the right to disposal of natural resources
and wealth is indirectly addressed to the exercise of the
right to nationalize or expropriate. This right is now
recognized as a legal exercise of sovereignty.(70) What is
debatable is the question of whether or not compensation
should be paid.(71)

The article goes on to urge states in Africa to
exercise this right either individually or collectively
with a view toward strengthening African unity and
solidarity. The OAU has, to some extent, addressed the
need to promote collective self-reliance as advocated in
this article. The most notable continental move in this
direction is the Lagos Plan of Action for Economic
Development of Africa adopted at the extraordinary meeting
of Heads of State and Government of the OAU in April 1980
in Lagos.(72) In addition, there are some subregional
economic initiatives worth noting. These include
ECOWAS,(73) SADCC,(74) and PTA.(75)

Article 21 also makes reference to the exploitation of
African wealth by foreigners, in particular the monopolies.
The charter urges the states to undertake the elimination
of all forms of foreign economic exploitation. This is of
particular interest because almost the whole African
economy is controlled by the powerful giant multinational
corporations from the West. Some of these are richer than
their hosts and in some cases determine what takes place in
these poor states.(76) This is sometimes done in collaboration or in conspiracy with corrupt and unpatriotic
elements in African countries who are prepared to sell
their countries' natural wealth in return for illicit
payments banked in numbered accounts abroad.(77)
Currently, the United Nations is in the process of
preparing a Code of Conduct on Transnational Corporations
in an attempt to tame them.(78) The reference to these
corporations in the African Charter on Human and People's
Rights is a recognition of their destructive nature to
young and weak economies.

Right to Development

The right to development in the African Charter on
Human and People's Rights fascinates many lawyers.(79)
This right, which is provided in Article 22, is also one
of the most prominent of the third generation of human
rights.

This right is central to the African understanding of
human rights in general. This comes clearly in the words
of Senghor: "Our overall conception of Human Rights is
remarked by the right to development since it integrates
all economic, social and cultural rights, and, also civil
and political rights. Development is first and foremost a
change of the quality of life and not only an economic
growth required at all costs, particularly in the blind
repression of individuals and peoples. It means the full
development of every man in his community."(80)

The duty to implement this right is placed upon the
states by the charter. This is because the struggle for

development is at various levels--international, regional, and national. At the international level it would involve working hand-in-hand in pursuit of the realization of strategies such as the New International Economic Order.

As Senghor correctly puts it, the form of development envisaged should be geared toward the welfare of the people in the society. It should not be development of things in the society which, in most cases, lead to high figures about development while people are starving. It should also be development in which people are fully participating. In no way should the fundamental freedoms be suspended for the sake of the so-called development. In this context, what Jack Donnelly observes about development in South Korea is relevant: "The ultimate purpose of development is to lay the basis for realizing human dignity...a strategy that assures material progress while precluding political participation, the enjoyment of civil rights and the unfolding of man's higher nature is incomplete, whatever its other attractions."(81)

That is a real conceptualization of the right to development. It makes little, if any, sense to have skyscrapers, industries, and other forms of general material well-being at the expense of freedom of the individual. That is not development but a new form of material enslavement.

The right to development also means the development of all the people in the society and not the creation of a small group of privileged persons who have everything at their disposal while the rest of the people are starving.(82) In other words, for the realization of this right, all the people should be assured of at least the basic human needs.

Right to International Peace and Security

There is no continent on earth that requires peace as urgently as Africa. Interstate and national conflicts on the continent are quite prevalent. While some of the conflicts are African in origin, most of them are instigated and fueled by forces beyond Africa. These forces range from private arms dealers to governments.(83)

Some of these forces against African peace and unity use the so-called "soldiers of fortune" (mercenaries) to destabilize various states on the continent. In the first 20 years of independence in Africa, from 1960 to 1980, mercenaries have been in action in more than fifteen African states.(84)

Currently, apart from South Africa, where there is almost a permanent state of emergency due to the oppressive and inhumane system of apartheid, there are ongoing conflicts in Angola, Chad, Burundi, Ethiopia, Mozambique, Namibia, Sahara Arab Democratic Republic, Sudan, and Uganda. Also, every government in power on the continent has an exiled opposition.

This grim picture indicates the importance of the right to peace and security to the people of Africa. This cannot be achieved through the invitation to superpowers to come and establish military bases on the continent, as

some countries have done.(85)   That just worsens the
situation.   The African people require total peace and
security in total freedom.
     In an attempt to ensure that one member to the charter
is not used as a source of problems to others, the charter
provides that a state shall not allow foreigners it has
granted asylum to use this hospitality for launching
attacks and engaging in other subversive activities against
their countries of origin.(86) In addition, a party shall
not allow its territory to be used for terrorist purposes
against other states.(87) This was included in the charter
because practice indicates that many states on the
continent allow opposition parties or groups from other
states to operate fully within their state.

                Right to a Satisfactory Environment

     Article 24 of the charter provides for a form of a
right which formerly was foreign to the continent, a right
that was not controversial at any level of discussion of
the charter.   That is the right to a clean environment
which is favorable to the development of the people of
Africa.
     Most of the discussions on environment on the
continent have centered on issues such as natural disasters
arising out of drought, floods, attacks by locusts, and
related problems.   Environmental problems arising out of
industrialization are still unknown to Africans due to lack
of serious industrial development. Most of the industries
existing on the continent from the colonial era to the
present are mainly import substitution facilities. There
are hardly any heavy industries.

     Export of Toxic Waste to Africa. Of late, however,
Africa has been attacked by an industrial-related plague:
the export of toxic industrial waste to the continent.
Suddenly, Africa has become the industrial world's dumping
ground.(88)
     Export of toxic waste in general has become a
lucrative international business.   The highly developed
countries in the world, particularly in the West, due to
the growth of powerful environmental lobbies, are finding
it more and more complicated to deal with their industrial
wastes.(89)   The solution has been to send these wastes
abroad.   The main victims are the poor countries of Eastern
Europe(90) and the Third World.(91)
     The reason for this export of toxic waste abroad,
which has been characterized as a new form of slavery,(92)
colonialism,(93) or poison tourism,(94) is purely economic.
Most of the exporters of industrial waste have the
technological means of effectively dealing with this poison
within their own boundaries. However, they allege that it
is too expensive to do so.   It is cheaper to export the
waste than treat it at home.(95) The high rates of profit
must be maintained.
     The export is done either openly, that is, with all
the parties involved knowing what is at stake, or

fraudulently, by one party (in most cases, the exporter) misrepresenting the nature of the cargo being exported to the unsuspecting importer.(96)

In Africa, toxic waste which is already threatening not only human and animal life but also vegetation is imported in two main forms. First, officially through governments which contract with firms abroad, and second, illegally through individuals privately contracting with firms from the exporting countries. These firms, most of which are merely "briefcase" or "postbox" firms with no fixed or permanent address, act for and on behalf of rich and influential clients who would not like to ruin their business good will.(97) We will examine some of the cases of acceptance of toxic waste on the continent, beginning with official and then moving to the illegal importation.

Toxic Waste Agreements with African States. At the moment four African states are known to have entered into agreements with foreign firms through which they have put their territories at the disposal of these firms as depositories for industrial toxic waste. These states are:

GUINEA BISSAU: In February 1988, the government of Guinea Bissau entered into a ten-year contract(98) with three European firms, namely, Bis Import-Export of London;(99) Hobday of the Isle of Man;(100) and Intercontrat of Fribourg, Switzerland. According to this contract, Guinea Bissau would, in the agreed period, take three million tons of toxic waste. The price would be $40 per ton or a total annual revenue of $120 million.(101) The waste is to be buried at two sites, Rio Geba and Farim, in the northwest of the country near the border with Senegal. All the costs of preparing the dumping sites and provision of suitable port facilities for the handling of the toxic waste would be met by the three companies. The task of dealing with the toxic cargo in Bissau has been subcontracted to a Portuguese company, Processamento de Residuos Industries.(102) In this contract, which was arranged through Robert Zeff, a Detroit-based lawyer,(103) Guinea Bissau was represented by Henrig Menezez d'Alva, the director of the Research and Applied Technologies Center of Guinea Bissau.(104)

BENIN: The most intriguing agreement was entered into between the government of Benin and SESCO, a British firm based in Gibraltar. AT the signing ceremony, Benin sent a high-powered delegation. It included the minister in the president's office in charge of planning and statistics, Mohammed Souradjou Ibrahim, and Finance Minister Barnabe Birdouzo. Mrs. Lamia Catche, the executive vice-president of a chemical handling firm, Hamilton Resources, signed on behalf of SESCO.

In this agreement, Benin accepted between one and five million tons of toxic waste for $2.50 per ton, plus 50 cents per ton to go toward a variety of development projects.(105) Ironically, the Benin officials praised the agreement as it would create about 200 jobs and generate about four billion CFA francs yearly. According to the parties, the agreement is supposed to be secret and confidential and its contents can only be revealed on the order of a court of law.(106)

Interestingly, Benin seems to have been so eager to get into the dumping business that in the beginning it was using its own merchant marine vessel, the Ganvie, to carry toxic waste into the country. This ceased following strong protests by the local dockers, who threatened that they would not handle toxic waste.(107)

EQUATORIAL GUINEA: In an agreement personally approved by President Teotoro Obiang Nguema Mbagoso, Equatorial Guinea allowed the British company Emvatrex to deposit about five million tons of toxic waste in a ten-year period in a 200-hectares piece of land on the island of Annobon.   In return, Equatorial Guinea was to receive a down-payment of $1.6 million.(108)   According to the director of Emvatrex, John Bevan, the government of Equatorial Guinea was enthusiastic about the agreement and was using convicts to prepare the site for the dumping of the waste.(109)

This agreement, like all the rest, has serious ecological consequences.   The island of Annobon, the deposit site, is of porous rock and there is a likelihood of toxic seepage which will damage Atlantic ecology, including some of Africa's richest fishing grounds.

CONGO: The Congolese agreement, which is now officially denied, was planned and organized by a Liechtenstein-based company, Bauwerk AG.   Its counterpart on the Congo side was Congolese Industrial Waste Recovery Company (CRDI), set up by Vincent Gomes, a lawyer, ostensibly with a go-ahead from high officials in the government.

For the purposes of acquiring toxic waste, Bauwerk's chief, Pessini Renato, subcontracted Export Waste Management, Inc., of New Jersey, and Van Santen BV of Moerdijk, Holland. The former was to handle business on the US side and the latter in Europe.

On the US side, there was absolutely no problem. Business was running as usual.   Export Waste Management, Inc., managed to acquire a clearance from the Environmental Protection Agency (EPA) and shipments from the ports of Savannah on the east coast and Richmond in California were in the final stages of preparation.   The problem arose from the European side.   Van Santen BV wanted to specialize in export of toxic waste from the Federal Republic of Germany.   The deal exploded when Van Santen BV's director, Theo Looschelder, who had an official import license from the Congolese authorities, attempted to get export clearance from the Netherland's Ministry of Environment.   Everything became public and this forced the Congolese regime to deny the agreement.(110)

In the panic and in an attempt to clear its name, the government sacked and arrested those alleged to have been involved in the agreement.   The affected persons include Dieudonne Ganga, and adviser in the prime minister's office, Issanga Gamissimi, Director of Environment, Abel Tchicou, Director of External Trade, Vincent Gomes (founder of CRDI and the alleged brain behind the deal), and Jean Passi, an artisan.

If the agreement had functioned, it would have lasted for three years and would have yielded about 1.2 billion

CFA francs for the Congo.(111)

   Toxic Waste Agreements with Private Individuals. The
second form of agreement on toxic wastes are those entered
into between private individuals in Africa and foreign
firms. The most prominent of these have been in Nigeria
and Guinea.
   The figure who appears in every piece of news on
export of toxic waste to Africa is that of Sunday Nana, a
Nigerian farmer who lives near the small port of Koko.(112)
The toxic waste exported to Nigeria came from Italy. The
private agreement was arranged by Gianfranco Raffaeli, an
Italian national who has lived and worked for many years as
a building contractor in Nigeria. It was through his
company, Iruekpen Construction Company, that the toxic
waste was imported.(113)
   Raffaeli and his associates agreed with Sunday Nana in
November 1987 that his company would use Nana's piece of
land near Koko to store toxic waste. The storage, which,
Nana was assured, was not dangerous, was to earn him about
500 Naira (about US$120) per month. It is when the first
load came that Nana and his neighbors started to sense
problems. A strong odor began coming from the drums
containing the waste. The smell was so strong that people
could no longer sleep.(114)
   Nigerian students in Pisa, Italy, wrote to alert their
government of the export of toxics into their country after
reading about it in the local newspaper, Il Mondo.(115)
Among the wastes exported to Nigeria were
polychlorinatedbiphenyls (PCB), one of the most dangerous
groups of chemical compounds in the world, polyurethanes,
ethyl acetate formaldehyde, and methyl melamine.
   On receipt of the letter from the students, the
Nigerian government acted swiftly. All those who had
collaborated with Raffaeli (who had meanwhile managed to
escape from the country) were immediately arrested. These
included Desi Derio Perazzi, the managing director of an
Italian company in Nigeria, and Poletti Construction
Company, which had assisted with the transport of the toxic
waste from the port of Koko into the town.
   In addition, Nigeria recalled its ambassador to Rome
and asked Italy to do the same to its chargé d'affaires in
Lagos, Gianfranco Colognato. The Nigerian authorities also
called upon the Italian government to remove the waste
deposited near Koko.
   It is said that the resolute action on this matter on
the part of the Nigerian government was prompted by the
great embarrassment it felt having championed the matter of
waste at a just-ended summit. During the OAU summit in
Addis Ababa in May 1988, Nigerian President Ibrahim
Babangida, in a morals-studded speech, told other African
leaders: "That any African state could collude with
industrial countries to dump nuclear waste on its territory
is not only shocking but incomprehensible. No government
has the right to mortgage the destiny of future generations
of African children to nuclear radiation."(116)
   It was therefore a shock to Babangida that what he had
just been condemning was to some extent happening on his

own soil.(117)

The second secret and private importation of toxic waste to Africa was in the Republic of Guinea. Here it was done by a semiofficial firm, the Guinea-Norwegian joint company Guinormar. The company had imported 15,000 tons of toxic waste from Philadelphia, in the United States, for which it was paid $50 per ton. The waste, which was falsely designated as raw materials for brick-making, was dumped at Kassa Island, near Conakry. The effects of the dumping were rather fast. The foul smell was intense and trees on the island began to dry up and die.

On discovering the illegal importation, the government arrested Norwegian Consular-General Sigmund Strome, who was also the managing director of Guinormar.(118)

Effects of the Export of Toxic Waste to Africa. Recent as it is, the export of toxic waste to Africa has had serious side effects on the continent, its people, and its politics. These effects are both positive and negative.

First, on the positive side, it has awakened environmental awareness in most people, not only in the areas affected but on the whole continent. In Benin, for example, it has led to the formation of Africa's first political opposition devoted primarily to ecological issues like most "Green" parties in Europe. The party, called Beninois pour la Libertė et la Democratie (MBLD), is led by Captain Adabaou Kossa, who says that President Kerekou of Benin has turned the country into "la poubelle de l'Africa" (the dustbin of Africa). In an interview with the BBC, the leader of the MBLD said that his movement will not allow one more ounce of waste to be buried in the Benin soil and that Kerekou will be the first head of state to fall victim to the well-organized ecological movement.(119)

Second, on the negative side, there are many side effects. Apart from the well-known dangers to life and vegetation, export of toxic waste to the continent will increase instability due to possibilities of clashes between states. Many states are likely to quarrel because of trans-frontier pollution arising out of dumping. There are already threats of clashes between Nigeria and Benin. Nigeria is said to have been extremely angered at the possibility that Benin might dump waste on the border between the two West African states. President Babangida made it clear to his counterpart in Benin that if that dumping took place, the Nigerian army "would descend on Cotonou."(120)

At the same time, dumping is going to interfere with attempts to have total peace on the continent, a situation which affects the people's right to peace. This is an alarming situation since there are reports that toxic waste is being accepted by some regimes in exchange for arms.

OAU and the Dumping of Toxic Waste in Africa. The OAU has officially condemned the importation of toxic waste to the continent. The antidumping declaration was part of a joint African statement to mark the 25th anniversary of the

organization.(121)
     The OAU Council of Ministers, in a strongly worded
resolution, declared the dumping of nuclear and industrial
wastes in Africa to be a crime against Africa and the
African people.(122) The resolution goes on to condemn all
transnational corporations and enterprises involved in the
introduction, in any form, of nuclear and industrial
wastes in Africa, and demands that they clean up the
areas that they have already contaminated.(123)
     Furthermore, the resolution calls upon African
countries which have concluded or are in the process of
concluding agreements for dumping nuclear and industrial
wastes in their territories to put an end to these
transactions, and above that, to carry out information
campaigns among their people about the danger of nuclear
and industrial wastes.
     In order to effectively combat dumping, the Council
of Ministers requested that the secretary-general of the
OAU, in close collaboration with the director-general of
the International Atomic Energy Agency (IAEA), the
executive secretary of the United Nations Economic
Commission for Africa (ECA), the executive director of the
United Nations Environmental Program (UNE), and other
concerned organizations, assist African countries to
establish appropriate mechanisms for monitoring and
controlling the movement and disposal of nuclear and
industrial waste in Africa. Also, the ministers requested
that the OAU secretary-general take appropriate steps to
ensure the inscription of the dumping of nuclear and
industrial wastes in Africa as an item on the agenda of the
43d Session of the UN General Assembly. This was done in
the hope that dumping in general and in Africa in
particular would receive international condemnation.(124)
     The OAU has also established a working group charged
with the drafting of a Convention on the Control of the
Movement of Dangerous Wastes Across Borders. It is hoped
after the recent experiences that this group is likely to
work fast and produce the much-awaited draft convention.
     It is, however, sad to note that the efforts by the
OAU are not finding much support and/or encouragement from
the countries from which nuclear and industrial wastes
come. For instance, while the European Economic Community
(EEC) agrees that the companies exporting toxic waste to
Africa are engaged in "morally reprehensible activities,"
it argues that they have, however, not broken any EEC rules
and cannot therefore be brought to justice.(125)
     The Netherland's environment minister, Ed Nijpels,
attempted to introduce a ban on export of toxic waste
during the meeting of the European Entente for the
Environment (EEE) Environment Ministers in Luxembourg on
June 29, 1988. Colin Moynihan, British Junior Minister for
Environment, blocked this move on the grounds that the
final choice about whether to accept the waste should be
left to the recipient state.(126)

IMPLEMENTATION OF PEOPLE'S RIGHTS IN TANZANIA

It is not easy to say with certainty that there has been a

conscious application of what are characterized as people's
rights in the African Charter on Human and People's Rights
in Tanzania. However, there have been measures, taken by
both the party and the government, which might be said to
reflect, support, or unconsciously implement people's
rights as they are provided for in the charter. We
examine some of these rights below.

First, equality of all people: notwithstanding its
failures elsewhere, the government of Tanzania has put
everything at its disposal to ensure that there is
equality of all people in the country. Tanzania is made up
of about 120 different nationalities with distinct
languages, customs, and cultures. However, conflict among
Tanzanians is completely foreign. They feel and actually
are ndugus (brothers). Religion, which is a potential
threat to unity in various states, plays an insignificant
role in everyday life in Tanzania. Muslims, Christians,
and believers of other religions live together without
tensions.(127)

Equality, which has been a source of peace and
stability, has come from the policy of the government
through which all people have been provided equal
opportunity, particularly in education. Other facilities
such as health and social amenities have also been easily
accessible to the masses. They have been either free or
subsidized to the extent that even the lower sections of
the population could easily afford them.(128)

However, everything seems to be changing slowly.
Since 1984 most of the policies of the government have been
constantly reviewed. This follows an agreement between the
government and the International Monetary Fund (IMF).(129)
As usual, the IMF has suggested its regular "medicine"--
structural adjustment of the economy.(130) Simply put,
that means the cutting of government expenditure on social
amenities to the people. Therefore, apart from the heavy
devaluation of the Tanzanian shilling,(131) the government
has now introduced fees on medical treatment(132) and fees
in all schools except the university.(133) It follows
therefore that only those who can afford it may have access
to these basic facilities. It also means that class
differentiation, which was there before, but not very
pronounced,(134) will now be consolidated and entrenched.
It also means that there will be a reproduction of well-
off citizens who will have total control of the state. In
other words, a new form of feudal system is likely to grow
up. That is, the son walks into the father's shoes because
the father had the means to prepare such a transition. In
this set-up the poor are condemned.

In addition, the way toward total disintegration of
the political system is paved by the tendency of
politicians to make laws which directly benefit them and to
a larger extent isolate them from the rest of the
population. This began in 1978 when the members of
parliament sat in Pemba and increased not only their own
salaries but also other benefits. This led to a mass
outcry and a demonstration by university students. The
government reacted sharply by expelling the students.(135)
But now the state in Tanzania seems to be completely immune
to any criticism. In 1981 it enacted a new law on pensions

for political leaders.(136) However, the most interesting
piece of legislation is the Specified State Leader
Retirement Benefits Act, 1986.(137) This act, which
applies to both mainland Tanzania and Zanzibar, provides
for retirement benefits for a former president, a former
vice-president, and a former prime minister.(138) The
above-mentioned leaders are given such terminal benefits
that their financial status after leaving office does not
change. While it has been said that this is done in order
to discourage top office holders in the country from
stealing public funds and banking them abroad for the
"rainy day" when they are no longer in power, the amount
awarded to these persons is absolutely disproportionate to
the real situation in the country. For example, a former
president receives, on retirement, a leadership gratuity of
Tshs. 3,105,000 and an annual pension of Tshs. 124,200,000
and both sums are tax-free.(139) This means that leaders
who have been preaching socialism throughout their
political careers suddenly become millionaires on
retirement. This is not easy to understand. As we have
indicated above, it only alienates the people from the
leaders. It is not easy to talk of equality in this
situation.

Equality of all the people, advocated by the African
Charter, will come when there is a total turnaround in
Tanzania. Its implementation is not likely to be
entertained in the near future.

Second, the right to self-determination: in connection
with this right, one can only discuss the position of
Tanzania on the liberation struggle in Africa and the world
at large, because internally, the issue of self-
determination does not apply. There are no disadvantaged
minorities who are struggling for self-determination within
the country.

The issue of self-determination arose briefly in 1983
during the debate on the amendment of the constitution in
connection with the union between Tanganyika and Zanzibar,
which together form Tanzania.(140) The issue was, however,
not pursued to its logical conclusion. The union remains a
sensitive issue due to many unclear issues about it. On
the one hand, the constitution provides that Tanzania is
one country, and on the other, we have a separate
government in Zanzibar with its own coat of arms,
constitution, courts of law, and similar institutions.
Whether Zanzibaris can claim the right to self-
determination or not remains a gray area in the law of
nations.

On the colonialism and the liberation struggle in
Africa, the government of Tanzania has played a role which
cannot be easily ignored in the history of the continent.
Since the 1960s, Tanzania has hosted many liberation
movements, particularly those fighting for independence in
central and southern Africa. Some are still around. The
government has therefore over the years provided both moral
and material support to freedom fighters. In addition,
Tanzania is a member of the Frontline States on the
struggle in southern Africa(141) and the OAU Liberation
Committee is based in Dar es Salaam.(142)

Third, control over natural resources and wealth:

unlike many regions on the continent, the government in Tanzania has almost total control over the natural wealth and resources of the country.

This follows the implementation of the Arusha Declaration of 1967. Through this document, the party instructed the government to ensure that the major means of production and exchange were placed in the hands of the people or their government. This was to occur, among other means, by nationalization of private enterprises belonging to both foreigners and citizens. These included such entities as banks, insurance firms, and import-export companies(143). Businesses hitherto held by private entities were taken over by public enterprises.(144)

This is another area where there are proposed changes by the government. Currently, there are debates in Tanzania as to whether or not it was wise to nationalize the major means of production and put them in the hands of the people. This has brought about an open tug-of-war between the government and the party. While the party would like to consolidate the Arusha Declaration philosophy and spirit, the government would like to return the nationalized firms to the private sector. It is alleged that these firms are not profitable.(145)

In its current pro-private enterprise spirit the government is engaged in a campaign to invite foreigners to invest in the country.(146) In the same vein, in his recent official visit to the Federal Republic of Germany, President Ali Hassan Mwinyi spent most of his stay attempting to assure investors that Tanzania was now safe to invest in and that apart from having no intentions of nationalizing private firms, his government was preparing a new investment code to protect investors.(147)

Though not admitted in official circles, the achievements of the last two decades, which saw the placement of the major means of production in the hands of the people and thereby ensured that the natural resources and wealth of the nation went directly or indirectly to benefit the people, will soon go down the drain.

Fourth, right to development: some of the issues pertaining to this right have already been discussed above in connection with the right to equality and the right to have control over natural resources. What is clear is the fact that currently there is no agreement in the country as to what development means. It is, however, a progressive change that at least the issue is being debated. That in itself is a process toward democratization of the society which is much needed on the continent.

The only disadvantage is that the debate is restricted to the high echelons of the government and the party. The average person on the street is not in a position to participate.

The point at issue is as follows: the party would like to see the continuation of the socialist policies it has advocated over the years. These policies, some of which we have discussed above, have their advantages and disadvantages. On the positive side, they have, among other things, managed to forge national unity.(148) The negative side has been the economy. The party seems not to have had a clear economic program. Its own general program

appeared for the first time in 1981.(149) While the Arusha
Declaration discussed at length the situation of the
economy, it underplayed the whole issue of industrialization of society.   This was catastrophic.   There have
been times when shops were empty and people had nothing to
eat or wear.   These incidents have been gold mines for
those making a case for the liberalization and privati-
zation of the economy and introduction of a full-fledged
capitalist system of development à la the IMF.   The people
are divided. On the one hand, they would not like to go
either hungry or naked. On the other hand, they know that
it helps little to have shops full of things which the
average person cannot afford.   It is argued that there is a
psychological satisfaction when people see full shops.
However, such satisfaction can neither fill an empty
stomach nor cover a naked body.
     Recently, the party came up with a sort of middle-way
solution.   It has directed that liberalization of the
economy should continue, but under the strict control of
the government.   Traders should import only essential
goods (goods which are likely to alleviate scarcity).
According to the party chairman, Nyerere, "some traders
have gone far off course, importing luxuries and useless
items such as tomato sauce and chocolates."(150) It will
be interesting to see what type of development is going to
take place in the country in the next few years.
     Fifth, peace and security: it could be said with
sincerity that there has generally been peace and security.
It is more peaceful than in most developed states where
the crime rate is higher.   People can usually go about
their business without harassment or molestation.   In
short, there is little fear for one's personal safety.
     There has been a new type of problem in the rural
areas.   Since the beginning of the 1980s there has been an
increase in the crime of cattle theft.(151)   Due to the
shortage of police and security personnel, it has not been
easy to completely eradicate this form of crime.   Being
desperate, peasants in the areas known to have many cattle
began to organize traditional defense forces.   These
forces, called Sungu Sungu, have now been recognized by the
party, and are widespread in the Mwanza, Shinyanga, and
Tabora regions.(152)
     Reading through the newspapers, one notices an
increase also in crimes related to the use of firearms,
including armed robbery.   This has also invaded Zanzibar,
where the rate of crime has generally been very low.   It is
suspected that the increase in crime is to some extent
related to liberalization of the economy. Inflation is high
and the shops are full of attractive items which most
persons cannot afford, hence the resort to crime.(153)
This is rather alarming in the commercial centers.
     Sixth, the right to a clean environment: the main
environmental problems in Tanzania have been noted as
drought, soil erosion, deforestation, poaching, infectious
and waterborne diseases, and bushfires.(154) There is also
the problem of water pollution, particularly along the 840
kilometers of coastline.(155)
     There are no clear-cut legal provisions which stand as
a guard against tampering with the environment.   One has

to examine various pieces of legislation which cover
matters related to the environment. These are laws dealing
with such topics as water, tourism, wildlife, land,
forestry, fishing, and natural resources. There are also a
few provisions in the penal law on crimes relating to
pollution of the environment. These are on water, air, and
noise.(156)

For a long time there has been no coherent national
policy on the environment in Tanzania. There have been
haphazard efforts by various ministries and institutions
within their restricted spheres of operation to deal with
particular aspects of the environment. Serious campaigns
have been launched particularly on soil conservation, which
arise mainly because of deforestation. This has been on
the increase because the majority of Tanzanians depend on
wood as fuel for both cooking and heating.

A new development came in 1983 with the establishment
of the National Environment Management Council.(157) The
council, which is a corporate body, has the task of
formulating policies on the environment and acting as an
advisory body to the government on all matters relating to
the environment.(158) The council is to operate closely
with other institutions dealing with environmental issues.
These include the National Land Use Planning Commission,
which was established in 1984 to advise the government on
all matters relating to land use.(159)

In the wake of export of toxic waste to Africa, the
council has been very active in ensuring that the calamity
does not reach Tanzania. Recently, the government formed a
task force under the coordination of the council to "guard
the country against the world problem of disposal of
hazardous wastes and radioactive substances imported from
abroad."(160) According to the director general of the
council, Ndugu Geogrey I. Kamukala, the task force will
have members from the Tanzania National Radiation
Commission, Tanzania Commission for Science and Technology,
Tanzania Bureau of Standards, Attorney-General's Chamber,
and Customs and Sales Department. There will also be
representatives from the ministries of health and social
welfare, foreign affairs, industries and trade, and the
Government Chemist Laboratory.(161) To advise the task
force will be experts from among other institutions, the
Faculty of Science, the Institute of Marine Sciences of the
University of Dar es Salaam, and the Tropical Pesticides
Research Institute.

Therefore, although developments in Tanzania
pertaining to the environment have been independent of the
African Charter on Human and People's Rights, it is most
likely that these efforts will, in the near future,
complement each other in an effort to ensure that all the
people of Africa can live and work in a clean and
satisfactory environment conducive to their development.

NOTES

1. This view is shared by many authors, including Wolfgang Benedek, "People's Rights and Individual's Duties as Special Features of the African Charter on Human and People's Rights," in Philip Kunig, Wolfgang Benedek, and Costa R. Mahalu, Regional Protection of Human Rights by International Law: The Emerging African Systems, pp. 59-90; Richard N. Kiwanuka, "The Meaning of 'People' in the African Charter on Human and People's Rights," American Journal of International Law 80 (1988), p. 80; and U. O. Umozurika, "The African Charter on Human and People's Rights," American Journal of International Law 77 (1983), p. 902.

2. The Universal Declaration on Human Rights of December 10, 1948, makes reference to "peoples" in the preamble but not in the operative text. The European Convention on Human Rights and the American Convention on Human Rights do not refer to "peoples" at all. This is also noted in Philip Kunig, "The Role of 'People's Rights' in the African Charter on Human and People's Rights," in K. Ginther and W. Benedek (eds.), New Perspectives and Conceptions of International Law: An Afro-European Dialogue (Vienna: Springer-Verlag, 1983), pp. 163-64.

3. See Richard N. Kiwanuka, "The Meaning of 'People' in the African Charter on Human and People's Rights," p. 82; W. Benedek, "People's Rights and Individual's Duties as Special Features of the African Charter on Human and People's Rights," p. 66; and Rose M. D'sa, "Human and People's Rights: Distinctive Features of the African Charter," Journal of African Studies 29 (1985), p. 77.

4. See A. G. Ringera, "The African Charter on Human and People's Rights: A Comment," The Advocate (Nairobi) 3 (1984), p. 15. Ringera argues among other things that the charter represents the maximum concession African states were willing to make on their jealously guarded sovereignties.

5. In international law, recognition of "people's" rights would entail reopening the debate over subjects and objects of international law. Traditionally, only states are subjects of international law. Kiwanuka makes casual reference to this point. See Richard N. Kiwanuka, "The Meaning of 'People' in the African Charter on Human and People's Rights."

6. Richard N. Kiwanuka, "The Meaning of 'People' in the African Charter on Human and People's Rights," p. 81.

7. W. Benedek, "People's Rights and Individual's Duties as Special Features of the African Charter on Human and People's Rights," p. 66.

8. On these rights, see Imre Szabo, "Fundamental Questions Concerning the Theory and History of Citizens' Rights," in Jozsef Halasz (ed.), Socialist Concept of Human Rights (Budapest: Akademiai Kiado, 1966), pp. 27-81; and Eberhard Poppe (ed.), Grundrechte des Burgers in der socialistischen Gesellschaft (Berlin: Staatsverlag der Deutchen Demokratischen Republik, 1980). The last source was brought to my notice by Dr. Wolfgang Kemnitzer of Martin Luther University, Hall (Saale), GDR.

9. See W. Benedek, "The Significance of the African Charter on Human and People's Rights for the Progressive Development of International Concept and Protection of

Human Rights" (mimeo.), a paper presented at a special conference on the African Charter on Human and People's Rights organized by the Gesellschaft für afrikanisches Recht (Heidelberg), July 3-4, 1987 at Limburg State University, Maastricht, Holland.

10. It is due to their insistence that Decision 115 (XVI) Rev. 1 of 1979 of Monrovia included the concept "peoples" in the document to be drafted by the group of experts.

11. Articles 19-24 of the African Charter on Human and People's Rights.

12. S. Palmeira, "The Principle of Self-Determination in International Law," International Association of Democratic Lawyers Review 1, no. 3 (1954).

13. D. B. Levin, "Self-determination of Nations in International Law," Soviet Yearbook of International Law, 1962, p. 46.

14. See the definition provided in G. Starushenko, The Principle of National Self-Determination in Soviet Foreign Policy (Moscow: Foreign Languages Publishing House, 1963), p. 169. See also the definition by Lenin, who says that the concept entails the political separation of colonial nations from alien national bodies and formation of an independent state. This is in V. I. Lenin, Critical Remarks on the National Question: The Right of Nations to Self-Determination (Moscow: Progress Publishers, 1971), p. 41.

15. U. O. Umozurike, Self-Determination in International Law (Hamden, Connecticut: Archon, 1972), p. 192.

16. See M. R. K. Rwelamira, "Contemporary Self-Determination and the United Nations Charter: An Appraisal of the Use of Force against Colonialism and Racial Discrimination in Southern Africa," African Review 6, no. 3 (1976).

17. See C. M. Peter, "The Right of Nations to Self-Determination in International Law: The Case of Western Sahara" (mimeo.), a dissertation submitted in partial fulfillment of the Degree of Master of Laws at the University of Dar es Salaam, Tanzania, 1984.

18. The Encyclopaedia Britannica, Volume 20 (1960), p. 306, for instance, says that "self-determination has become, since the American and the French revolutions a political, if not a legal principle expressing the right of a nation to form a government of its own choice. See also U. O. Umozurike, Self-Determination in International Law; M. A. Shukri, The Concept of Self-Determination in the United Nations (Damascus: Al Jadidah Press, 1965), p. 19; Clyde Eagleton, "Self-Determination and the United Nations," American Journal of International Law 47 (1953), p. 88; and A. Rigo-Sureda, The Evolution of the Right to Self-Determination (Leiden: A. W. Sijhoff, 1973).

19. Currently, control of weaker states is done through the agency of investors and in particular the giant multinational corporations. These firms interfere directly with the internal affairs of the hosts. In Gutto's words: "It should be recognized that foreign investors are inherently part and parcel of the political economies within which they operate. To say that they should not

"intervene" in the internal affairs of the countries they
operate in is absurd and demonstrates the nature of legal
thinking that fails to recognize the integrated nature of
foreign capital. See S. B. O. Gutto, "Responsibility and
Accountability of States, Transnational Corporations and
Individuals in the Field of Human Rights and Social
Development: A Critique," Third World Legal Studies
Association--Human Rights and Development (1984), pp 180-
81.

20. On these resolutions and the whole concept of
Permanent Sovereignty over Natural Resources, see George
Elian, The Principle of Sovereignty over Natural Resources
(Alphen aan den Rijn: Sijthoff & Noordhoff, 1979); and
Kamal Hossain and Subrata Roy Chowohury (eds.) Permanent
Sovereignty over Natural Resources in International Law:
Principle and Practice (New York: St. Martin's Press,
1984).

21. On the New International Economic Order, see,
inter alia, Mohammed Bedjaoui, Towards a New International
Economic Order (New York: Holmes & Meier, 1979), and Linus
A. Hoskins, The New International Economic Order: A
Bibliographic Handbook (Washington, D.C.: University Press
of America, 1982).

22. On this resolution, see R. F. Meagher, An
International Redistribution of Wealth and Power: A Study
of the Charter of Economic Rights and Duties of States (New
York: Pergamon, 1979).

23. This concept, coined by Karel Vasak, former
director of the International Institute of Human Rights at
Strasbourg, France, is discussed infra.

24. See Georges Abi-Saab, "The Right to Development on
the Universal and the African Levels" (mimeo.), 1987.

25. Actually, there have been attempts to trace the
origin of the right to development back to the American
Declaration of Independence and the French Declaration of
the Rights of Man and the Citizen. See the report of a
UNESCO working group of nongovernmental organizations,
"The Right of Solidarity: An Attempt at Conceptual
Analysis, UNESCO Doc. SS-80/Conf.806/6, July 9, 1980,
paragraph 36.

26. Part of this report titled "Le droit des peuples
sous developpe au developpement" is reproduced in J. R.
Dupuy (ed.), "The Right to Development at the International
Level," a report of a workshop held at the Hague Academy
of International Law, The Hague, October 16-18, 1979.

27. See Keba Mbaye, "Le droit au developpement comme
un droit de l'homme," Revue des droits de l'homme/ Human
Rights Journal 5, nos. 2-3 (1972).

28. See Keba Mbaye, "We Have to Fight More and More
for the Right to Development," The Courier (111),
September-October 1988, p. 2.

29. Vasak launched this concept in his article "Human
Rights: A Thirty-Year Struggle," UNESCO Courier, November
1977. Since then this concept has gained wide acceptance
in human rights circles. See also P. Alson, "Development
and the Rule of Law: Prevention versus Cure as a Human
Rights Strategy," in International Commission of Jurists,
Development, Human Rights and the Rule of Law (Oxford:
Pergamon, 1981), p. 101.

30. General Assembly Resolution 33/73 of 1978.
31. This resolution was highly influenced by the report of the UN secretary-general titled "The International Dimensions of the Right to Development as a Human Right in Relation with Other Human Rights based on International Cooperation, Including the Right to Peace, Taking into Account the Requirement of the New International Economic Order and Fundamental Needs, UN DOC.E/CN. 4/1334 of January 2, 1979.
32. Notwithstanding the popularity of this right, there is also opposition and criticism. See for instance Jack Donnelly, "The 'Right to Development': How Not to Link Human Rights and Development," in C. E. Welch, Jr. and R. I. Meltzer (eds.), Human Rights and Development in Africa, p. 261.
33. See the Preamble to the United Nations Charter.
34. For most of these documents, see Ian Brownlie (ed.) Basic Documents on Human Rights.
35. See Article 23, which will be elaborated later.
36. See Alexandre Kiss, "The International Protection of the Environment," in R. St. J. MacDonald and Johnston D. M. Douglas (eds.), The Structure and Process of International Law: Essays in Legal Philosophy, Doctrine and Theory (The Hague: Martinus Nijhoff, 1983), p. 1069.
37. See for instance the International Convention for the Protection of Birds, Paris, October 18, 1950.
38. On the international protection of animals, see for example the Convention for the Regulation of Whaling, Geneva, September 24, 1931, and the International Convention for the Regulation of Whaling, Washington, D.C. December 2, 1946.
39. See the Convention on Nature Protection and Wild Life Preservation in the Western Hemisphere, Washington, D.C., October 12, 1940.
40. See for example the various agreements entered into between and among African states on joint use of shared rivers which are dealt with at length in Bonaya Adhi Godana, Africa's Shared Water Resources: Legal and Institutional Aspects of Nile, Niger and Senegal River Systems (London: Frances Pinter Publishers, 1985). Also relevant are J. Symonides, "International Legal Problems of the Fight against Pollution of Rivers, Polish Yearbook of International Law 5 (1972-73) and Aziza M. Fahmi, "The Degree of Effectiveness of International Law as Regards International Rivers," Österreichische Zeitschrift für Offentliches Recht und Völkerrect 28 (1977).
41. See for example the Agreement Concerning the Navigation of Lake Constance, June 1, 1973, which is partly reproduced in Karin Oellers-Frahm and Norbert Wuhler (eds.), Dispute Settlement in Public International Law: Texts and Materials (Berlin: Springer Verlag, 1984), pp. 599-601. See also R. Zacklin and L. Caflisch (eds.), The Legal Regime of International Rivers and Lakes (The Hague: Martinus Nijhoff, 1981); P. H. Sand, "Development of International Law in the Lake Chad Development Basin," Zeitschrift für ausländisches Recht und Völkerrect 34 (1974); C. O. Okidi, "Legal and Policy Regime of Lake Victoria and Nile Basins," Indian Journal of International Law 20 (1980); and H . L. Dickstein, "International Lake

and River Pollution Control: Questions of Method," Columbia Journal of Transnational Law 12, 1954.

42. See the International Convention for the Prevention of the Pollution of the Sea by Oil, London, May 12, 1954.

43. See Bo Johnson, International Environmental Law (Stockholm: Liber Forlag, 1976), p. 21.

44. On the origin and functions of the UNEP, see Michael Hardy, "The United Nations Environment Program," in Ludwik A. Teclaff and Albert E. Utton (eds.), International Environmental Law (New York: Praeger, 1974), p. 57; and M. F. Strong, "A Global Imperative," in T. C. Emmel (ed.), Global Perspective for Ecology (Palo Alto, CA: Mayfield, 1977), Chapter 33.

45. See principle 21 of the conference in UN DOC. A/Conf. 48/14 of 1972.

46. Article 30 of General Assembly Resolution 3281 (XXIX) of December 1981. This resolution is reproduced in R. F. Meagher, An International Redistribution of Wealth and Power: A Study of the Charter of Economic Rights and Duties of States.

47. See Part XII titled "Protection and Conservation of the Marine Environment," which contains Articles 192-237. This convention, which is yet to come into force, is reproduced in Myron H. Nordquist (ed.), United Nations Convention on the Law of the Sea: A Commentary Volume 1 (Dordrecht: Martinus Nijhoff, 1985).

48. See World Commission on Environment and Development, Our Common Future (Oxford: Oxford University Press, 1988).

49. See J. Omo-Fadaka, "Brundtland's Environment Imperative," New African, no. 248 (May 1988).

50. See Rene Cassin, "Introduction: The International Law of Human Rights, Recuels des cours 144 (1974). This important statement is also quoted in W. P. Gormley, Human Rights and Environment: The Need for International Cooperation (Leiden: A. W. Sijhoff, 1976), p. 1.

51. It is particularly so in cases of the right to self-determination whose enjoyment requires a collective form of the people involved.

52. Address by Senghor to the Dakar meeting of African experts drafting the African Charter of Human and People's Rights, November 28, 1979.

53. A. M. Babu, African Socialism or Socialist Africa (London: Zed, 1981), p. 58.

54. Article 19.

55. Article 20.

56. Article 21.

57. Article 22.

58. Article 23.

59. Article 24.

60. Clashes among opposed nationalities have been taking place from time to time in Burundi, for example. The latest occurrence was in August 1988 in which thousands lost their lives. On this, see John Sweeney, "Revenge of the 'Tall Men'," Observer, September 4, 1988; "Terroristen in Burundi verübten die Massaker," no. 206 Die Welt, September 3, 1988; Gunter Krabbe, "Die Wiederholung des biblischen Kampfes zwischen viehzuchtenden Tutsi und

ackerbauenden Hutu in Burundi," no. 204, Frankfurter
Allgemeine Zeitung, September 2, 1988, p. 5; and Nancy
Hynes, "Donors Ponder Tribal Massacres," no. 122, African
Business, October 1988, p. 37. On the earlier clashes, see
Bruno Holtz, Burundi: Völkermord oder Selbstmord?
(Freiburg: Imba Verlag, 1973); and Stanley Meisler,
"Holocaust in Burundi, 1972," in Willem A. Veenhoven (ed.),
Case Studies on Human Rights and Fundamental Freedoms: A
World Survey (The Hague: Martinus Nijhoff, 1976), p. 225.
    61. A clear case is the Sudan, where the southern part
is engaged in a war with the central government due to,
among other reasons, racial discrimination against the
blacks in this area by the Arabs in the north. On the
civil war in the Sudan see inter alia M. K. Nduru, "SPLA
Rule Southern Airwaves," no. 245 New African, February
1988; Joseph Oduho and William Deng, The Problem of the
Southern Sudan (London: Oxford University Press, 1963); and
Edgar O'Ballance, The Secret War in the Sudan (London:
Faber & Faber, 1977).
    62. Recent reports indicate reemergence of slavery in
the Sudan and Mauritania, particularly involving black
women and children. See "Sudan: Rückfall in die
Sklaverei," no 50, Der Spiegel, December 7, 1987, p. 145,
and "Mauretanien: Walo Walo--Zum ersten Male versuchten die
Schwarzen einen Staatsstreich gegen die maurische
Oberschicht," no. 52, Der Speigel, December 21, 1987, p.
124. See also Claire C. Robertson (ed.), Women and Slavery
in Africa (Madison: University of Wisconsin Press, 1984).
    63. On the Nigerian civil war, see Jean Buhler,
Biafra: Tragödie eines begabten Volkes (Zurich: Schweizer
Spiegel Verlag, 1968); Tilman Zulch and Klaus Guerke
(eds.), Soll Biafra überleben? Documente--Berichte--
Analysen--Kommentare (Berlin: Lettner Verlag, 1969); Gustav
Seeburg, Die Wahrheit über Nigeria/Biafra: Vorgeschichte
und Hintergrunde des Konfliktes (Bern: Verlag Paul Haupt,
1969); and John J. Stremlau, The International Politics of
the Nigerian Civil War, 1967-1970 (Princeton: Princeton
University Press, 1977).
    64. See the Convention on the Prevention and
Punishment of the Crime of Genocide of 1948, which was
adopted by the United Nations General Assembly on December
9, 1948 and came into force in 1951. This document is
reproduced in American Journal of International Law 45
(Supplement) 1951, p. 7. Part of it is reproduced in D. J.
Harris, Cases and Materials on International Law, 3d ed.
(London: Sweet and Maxwell, 1983), p. 561.
    65. See S. Kwaw Nyameke Blay, "Changing African
Perspectives on the Right to Self-Determination in the Wake
of the Banjul Charter on Human and People's Rights, Journal
of African Studies 29 (1985), p. 147.
    66. See Articles 1(2) and 55.
    67. See Article 1 of the Additional Protocol 11
relating to the Protection of Victims of Non-International
Armed Conflicts adopted on June 8, 1977 in Geneva. This
protocol is reproduced in full in Dietrich Schindler and
Jiri Toman (eds.), The Law of Armed Conflicts: A Collection
of Conventions, Resolutions and other Documents, (Alphen
aan den Rijn: Sijthoff & Noordhoff, 1981). See also Geza
Herczegh, Development of International Humanitarian Law

(Budapest: Akademiai Kiado, 1984), Chapter 7.

68. This sub-article, which contains one of the basic principles of the OAU, is discussed in A. Bolaji Akinyemi, "The Organization of African Unity and the Concept of Non-Interference in the Internal Affairs of Member-States," British Yearbook of International Law 46 (1972-73), p. 393.

69. See infra for the development of this principle.

70. Anything done by a state in exercise of this right cannot be questioned elsewhere. This comes out clearly in the judgment of Chief Justice Fuller in Underhill vs. Hernandez (1897), 168, US 250, who said at 250 that "Every sovereign State is bound to respect the independence of every other State, and the Courts of one country will not sit in judgment of another done within its own territory." This holding was upheld in Banco Nacional de Cuba vs. Sabbatino (1964), 376 US 398. Also, see Michael Zander, "The Act of State Doctrine," American Journal of International Law 53 (1959), p. 826.

71. On various positions on this matter, see Hawa Sinare, Legal and Economic Effects of Expropriation and Nationalization of Foreign Investments (Constance: Wolfgang Haltung-Gorre Verlag, 1983); M. Sornarajah, The Pursuit of Nationalized Property (Dordrecht: Martinus Nijhoff, 1986); Francesco Francioni, "Compensation for Nationalization of Foreign Property: The Borderline between Law and Equity," International and Comparative Law Quarterly 24 (1975); Georg Schwarzenberger, International Law, Volume 1 (London: Stevens and Sons, 1976); and D. P. O'Connel, International Law, 2nd ed., Volume 1 (London: Stevens and Sons, 1970).

72. On the Lagos Plan of Action, see Umesh Kumar, "African Response to the International Economic Order: Lagos Plan of Action and Preferential Trade Area Treaty for the Eastern and Southern African States," Jahrbuch für afrikanisches Recht/ Yearbook for African Law 5 (1984), p. 81; John Ravenhill, "Collective Self-Reliance or Collective Self-Delusion: Is the Lagos Plan a Viable Alternative?" in Africa in Economic Crisis (London: Macmillan, 1986); and Adebayo Adedeji and Timothy M. Shaw (eds.), Economic Crisis in Africa: African Perspective on Development Problems and Potentials (Boulder, Colorado: Lynne Rienner, 1985)--Part I entitled "Self-Reliance and Self-Sustainment" deals entirely with the Lagos Plan of Action.

73. On the ECOWAS, see Peter Robson, Integration, Development and Equity: Economic Integration in West Africa (London: George Allen & Unwin, 1983); Douglas Rimmer, The Economies of West Africa (New York: St. Martin's Press, 1984); A. Owosekun, "Some Thorny Issues in the Economic Community of West Africa," in W. A. Ndongko (ed.), Economic Cooperation and Integration in Africa (Dakar: CODESRIA, 1985); and S. A. Olandrewaju and Toyin Falola, "Development through Integration: The Politics and Problems of ECOWAS," in Olusola Akinrinade and J. Kurt Barling (eds.), Economic Development in Africa: International Efforts, Issues and Prospects (London: Pinter, 1987).

74. On SADCC, see Samir Amin, Derrick Chitala, and Ibbo Mandaza (eds.), SADCC: Prospects for Disengagement and Development in Southern Africa (London: Zed, 1987); Douglas G. Anglin, "SADCC after Nkomati," African Affairs 84, no.

335 (1984), p. 163; Peter Meynes, "Southern African Development Coordination Conference (SADCC) and Regional Cooperation in Southern Africa," in Domenico Mazeo (ed.), Southern Africa: Toward Economic Liberation (London: Rex Collings, 1981); and "SADCC: Roadshow without Cast," Africa Confidential 24(2), January 19, 1983.

75. See Ngila Mwase, "The African Preferential Trade Area: Towards a Sub-Regional Economic Community in Eastern and Southern Africa," Journal of World Trade Law 19 (1985), p. 622; Hawa Sinare, "The Implication of the Preferential Trade Area for Economic Integration in Eastern and Southern Africa," in Ibrahim S. R. Msabaha and Timothy M. Shaw (eds.), Confrontation and Liberation in Southern Africa: Regional Directions after the Nkomati Accord (Boulder, Colorado: Westview, 1987), p. 157.

76. This point is made well by the former president of Tanzania, Julius Nyerere: "There is no such thing as a national economy at all! Instead, there exist [in a developing country] various economic activities which are owned by people outside its jurisdiction, which are directed at external needs and which are run in the interests of external powers. Further, the government's ability to secure positive action in these fields...depends entirely upon its ability to convince the effective decision-makers that their own interests will be served by what the government wishes to have done."

This was in an address to a convocation of Ibadan University in Nigeria in November 1976. Part of the address is reproduced in D. W. Nabudere, Essays on the Theory and Practice of Imperialism (London: Onyx Press, 1979), pp. 90-91; and Omwony-Ojwok, "Who is to Lead the Popular Anti-Imperialist Revolution in Africa: In Refutation of Issa G. Shivji's Petty-Bourgeois Neo-Marxist Line," in Yash Tandon (ed.), Debate on Class, State and Imperialism (Dar es Salaam: Tanzania Publishing House, 1982).

77. This happens not only in Africa but in developing countries elsewhere. A well-known case is that of the Philippines under now-deposed President Ferdinand Marcos. See L. B. Francisco and J. S. Fast, Conspiracy for the Empire: Big Business, Corruption and the Politics of Imperialism in America 1876-1907 (Quezon City: Foundation for Nationalist Studies, 1985); "How to Spend a Billion: Imelda Marcos Squandered Her Country's Money and Her Own Reputation,": Newsweek (US), March 24, 1986; and Lance Morrow, "Essay: The Shoes of Imelda Marcos," Time (US), March 31, 1986, p. 30.

78. On the draft Code of Conduct on Transnational Corporations, still under preparation, see A. A. Fatouros, "The UN Code of Conduct of Transnational Corporations: Problems of Interpretation and Implementation," in Seymour J. Rubin and Gary Clyde Hufbauer (eds.), Emerging Standards of International Trade and Investment (New York: West, 1985), p. 101, and Ebenroth Carsten-Thomas, Code of Conduct--Ansätze zur Verträglichen Gestaltung Internationaler Investitionen (Constance: Universitätsverlag Konstanz, 1987).

79. Currently, there is a lot being written on this. See for instance Mohammed Bedjaoui, "Right to Development and Jus Cogens," in Milan Bulajic, Dimitrije Pindic, and Momirka Marinkovic (eds.), The Charter of Economic Rights and Duties of States: Ten Years of Implementation (Belgrade: Institute of International Politics and Economy, 1986), p. 43; Emanuel De Kadt, "Some Basic Questions on Human Rights and Development," World Development 8 (1980), p. 97; Upendra Baxi, "The New International Economic Order, Basic Needs and Rights: Notes towards Development of the Right to Development," Indian Journal of International Law 23 (1983), p. 225; and C. G. Weeramantry, "The Right to Development," Indian Journal of International Law 25 (1985), p. 482.

80. Speech to the meeting of experts.

81. See Jack Donnelly, "Human Rights and Development: Complementary or Competing Concerns?" in G. W. Shepherd, Jr., and V. P. Nanda (eds.), Human Rights and Third World Development (Westport, Connecticut: Greenwood, 1985), p. 48.

82. For example, one of the reasons for the fall of the late Emperor Haile Selassie of Ethiopia was total disregard for the welfare of the people of Ethiopia. While millions were dying of hunger, the international press was displaying pictures of the emperor feeding his horses grain. On his downfall, see Colin Legum, Ethiopia: The Fall of Haile Selassie's Empire (London: Rex Collings, 1975); John Markakis and Nega Ayele, Class and Revolution in Ethiopia (Nottingham: Spokesman, 1978); Mulatu Wubneh and Yohanis Abate, Ethiopia: Transition and Development in the Horn of Africa (Boulder, Colorado: Westview, 1988); Heinz Gstrein, Athiopien blickt in die Zukunft (Freiburg: Imba Verlag, 1975); and Christian Potyka, Haile Selassie: der Negus Negesti in Frieden und Krieg (Bad Honnef: Osang Verlag, 1974).

83. See Wolfgang Benedek, "People's Rights and Individual's Duties as special Features of the African Charter on Human and People's Rights," p. 83.

84. On the destabilization of Africa through mercenaries, see C. M. Peter, "Mercenaries and International Humanitarian Law," Indian Journal of International Law 24, no. 3 (1984), pp. 382-89.

85. Kenya, for instance, concluded a treaty with the United States in 1980 in which, in return for expanded economic and military aid, Kenya was to provide the United States with access to air and naval facilities in its territory. See David F. Gordon, "Foreign Relations: Dilemmas of Independence and Development," in Joel D. Barkan (ed.), Politics and Public Policy in Kenya and Tanzania rev. ed. (New York: Praeger, 1984); and David Gordon, Journal of African Marxists, "Independent Kenya" (London: Zed, 1982); and Ngugi wa Thiong'O, Detained: A Writer's Prison Diary (London: Heinemann, 1981), p. 59.

86. Article 23(2)(a).

87. Article 23(2)(b).

88. See Francois Misser, "Africa: The Industrial World's Dumping Ground?" African Business, no. 119 (July 1988), p. 10.

89. The growth of environmentally oriented parties in Europe and elsewhere in the developed world is also partly due to the now frequent industrial accidents that extensively damage the environment. These parties (some of which are represented in parliaments) include: the Greens (Federal Republic of Germany); Les Verts and Les Verts-Parti Ecologiste (France); Ecology Party (Great Britain); Conhaontas Glas (Ireland); The Green Party (Canada); Dei Greng Alternative (Luxemburg); Miljo Partiet (Sweden); Committee of Correspondence (US); and Agelev and Ecolo (Belgium). See C. Spretnak, Die Grünen: Nicht links nicht rechts sondern vorne (Munich: Wilhelm Goldmann Verlag, 1985).

90. Notwithstanding their political differences, one of the most lucrative businesses between East and West is the sale of industrial waste. The Federal Republic of Germany, for example, finds it more convenient to export its waste to the German Democratic Republic than to treat it at home. This is because one ton of toxic waste costs about 3,400 Deutschmarks (DM) to treat, while the same amount of waste can be shipped to the GDR for 400 DM. Toxic wastes from the West go to other destinations in the East, too, including Romania. See Christian Grefe, "Gift für die Welt: Die Industriestaaten exportieren Ihr Sondermullproblem, stat es zu Hause zu lösen," no. 32, Die Zeit, August 5, 1988, p. 10.

91. Greenpeace studies indicate that there have been about 115 shipments of toxic waste during the last two years to several destinations in Africa and Latin America. The countries outside Africa which have been named include Mexico, Argentina, Brazil, Panama, and Uruguay. See Khor Kok Peng "Spilling the Beans on Toxic Waste Racketeers," Sunday News (Tanzania), October 2, 1988, p. 5.

92. See "Giftmull: Neue Sklaverei," no. 24, Der Spiegel, June 13, 1988, p. 147.

93. See Christian Grefe, "Gift für die Welt: Die Industriestaaten exportieren Ihr Sondermullproblem, stat es zu Hause zu lösen," p. 10.

94. Ibid.

95. Ibid.

96. This took place recently in Turkey. Here a German company called Weber, on behalf of its rich clients, Siemens, Bosch, and Daimler-Benz, exported 1,500 tons of toxic waste to Turkey in July 1988, alleging that it was raw materials for a cement factory in Goltas. On examination of the cargo of the carrier, Mv. Niktis Trader, by Turkish customs officers, it was discovered that the cargo had nothing to do with the cement factory. After discovering that the cargo contained dangerous chemicals, the ship was not allowed to unload. The Turkish minister of environment, Adnan Kahveci, characterized the whole affair as "toxic mafia from developed countries." See "Giftchronik," Tageszeitung, August 22, 1988, p. 3.

97. Most of these dubious companies are registered in places where registration and other business formalities are relaxed. These places include Gibraltar, Monaco, Bahamas, and Liechtenstein.

98. This contract was concluded, notwithstanding strong protest from the minister of health of Guinea Bissau, Andre Atchade. In a confidential memorandum to his president, the minister warned that the contract represented a threat to the security of the resources and the people. He argued further that there was a great risk of radioactive pollution which would contaminate surface and subterranean water. He also noted that even a small rumor of pollution would be sufficient to threaten the country's tourist industry. See no. 94, South (London), August 1988, p. 38.

99. Bis Import-Export has only one director, Anthony Cohen, of Stanmore, London. Cohen, who is an accountant by profession, denies any connection with the company, for which he prepared all administrative papers for the purpose of registration. See no. 94, South (London), August 1988.

100. The directors of this company are hard to trace. They include Martin John Gibbs and his wife, Margaret, whose last known address was in Cyprus but are said to have now moved to Gibraltar. See Alan George, "False Scent on Trail," no. 94, South (London), August 1988, p. 39.

101. See Francois Misser, "Africa: The Industrial World's Dumping Ground?" and Jato Thompson "Laying Africa Waste," no. 252, New African, September 1988, p. 35.

102. It is interesting to note that the above firms are just acting as "fronts" representing other large companies based elsewhere in developed countries. For example, the European Economic Community's chairman of Entente Europeene pour l'Environnement (EEE), Francois Ruelants du Vivier, who had access to the agreement between Guinea Bissau and these companies, alleges that the managers of Hopday and Bis Import-Export were acting as intermediaries for a US firm, Lindaco, of Detroit, which had applied to the US Environmental Protection Agency (EPA) in early 1988 for permission to export 15 million tons of toxic waste to Guinea Bissau. Also, Intercontrat, which is owned by Gian Franco Ambrosini, is known to act for other firms. In early 1987, this company attempted to export 2,100 tons of toxic waste containing high levels of cyanide and dioxine from the Italian company Jelly Wax, to Djibouti. However, the authorities in Djibouti refused to accept the waste. The ship carrying the waste, Mv. Zanoobia, went around the world with its cargo and was rejected in all countries it visited, including Venezuela, Greece, and Syria. It returned to Italy. On this, see "Giftmull: Neue Sklaverei," no. 24, Der Speigel, June 13, 1988, p. 147.

103. See Christian Grefe, "Gift für die Welt: Die Industriestaaten exportieren Ihr Sondermullproblem, statt es zu Hause zu lösen."

104. See Francois Misser, "Africa: The Industrial World's Dumping Ground?"

105. See Jato Thompson, "Laying Africa Waste."

106. See Francois Misser, "Africa: The Industrial World's Dumping Ground?"

107. See Paul Michaud, "Toxic Terrorists Dump Waste Off-Shore," New African 251 (August 1988), p. 15.

108. See Francois Misser, "Africa: The Industrial World's Dumping Ground?"

109. Ibid.
110. See "Giftmull: Neue Sklaverei."
111. See Jato Thompson, "Laying Africa Waste."
112. See Patrick Smith and Alan George, "The Dumping Grounds," South (London) 94 (August 1988), p. 38; "Giftmull: Neue Sklaverei," no. 24, Der Speigel, 1988, p. 147; and Peter Ezeth, "Nigerians Who Stole Toxic Waste," New African 253 (October 1988), p. 22.
113. This company was established on July 26, 1976 as Pebulafia Construction Company and changed its name in 1978.
114. See "Giftmull: Neue Sklaverei."
115. See Jato Thompson, "Laying Africa Waste."
116. See Nicholas Woodsworth, "Lagos Protests to Rome on Toxic Waste," Financial Times, June 9, 1988.
117. See Geoffrey Lean and Eileen MacDonald, "Poison Cargo: Britain's Dirty Business," Observer, September 4, 1988, p. 15.

118. See Christian Grefe, " Gift für die Welt: Die Industriestaaten exportieren Ihr Sondermullproblem, statt es zu Hause zu lösen"; Khor Kok Peng, "Spilling the Beans on Toxic Waste Racketeers."
119. See Paul Michaud, "Toxic Terrorists Dump Waste Off-Shore."
120. Ibid.
121. See Victor Mallet, "Dumping in Africa Condemned," Financial Times, May 26, 1988.
122. See Resolution CM/Res. 1153 (XLVIII) of the 48th session held in Addis Ababa, May 19-23, 1988.
123. Ibid.
124. We are grateful to Mr. Elikundi E. E. Mtango, minister-chancellor at the Permanent Mission of the United Republic of Tanzania to the United Nations in Geneva for facilitating our acquisition of this resolution and other documents on the OAU.
125. See Shade Islam and Patrick Smith, "Dirty Games in Brussels," South 94 (August 1988), p. 41.
126. Ibid. This is surprising because most of the developed states have strict rules on toxic and related wastes and regard the whole question of wastes as a big challenge. See Christoph Harris et al, Hazardous Waste: Confronting the Challenge (New York: Quorum Books, 1987); Michael Greenberg and Richard F. Anderson, Hazardous Waste Sites: The Credibility Gap (New Brunswick, N .J.: Rutgers University Press, 1984); and John P. Lehman (ed.), Hazardous Waste Disposal (New York: Plenum Press, 1983).
127. The only religious incident which nearly disrupted national unity occurred in 1959. During the struggle for independence, some conservative Muslim leaders in the coast region, operating through the All Muslim National Union of Tanganyika (AMNUT) proposed to the colonial government that Tanganyika's independence should be delayed until Muslims had achieved educational equality with Christians. This proposal was vetoed by some progressive sheikhs. See John Iliffe, A Modern History of Tanganyika (Cambridge: Cambridge University Press, 1979), pp. 551-52; and also C. M. Peter, "Justice in a One-Party African State: The Tanzanian Experience--A Rejoinder,"

Verfassung und Recht in Übersee 20, no. 2 (1987), p. 239.
128. On some of the policies of the government of
Tanzania, see Andre Coulson (ed.), African Socialism in
Practice: The Tanzanian Experience (Nottingham: Spokesman,
1979); Andrew Coulson, Tanzania: A Political Economy; C.
George Kahama et al., The Challenge for Tanzania's Economy
(London: James Currey, 1986); M. Von Freyhold, Ujamaa
Villages in Tanzania: Analysis of a Special Experiment
(London: Heinemann Educational Books, 1979); Rodger Yeager,
Tanzania: An African Experiment (Boulder, Colorado:
Westview, 1982); Idrian A. Resnick, De Long Transition:
Building of Socialism in Tanzania (New York: Monthly Review
Press, 1981); Nyerere, J. K. Bilding und Beifreiung
(Frankfurt: Verlag Otto Lembeck, 1977).
129. See Kighoma A. Malima, "IMF and the World Bank
Conditionality: The Tanzanian Case," in Peter Lawrence,
(ed.) World Recession and the Food Crisis in Africa
(London: James Currey, 1985), pp. 129-39.
130. The policy of the IMF in developing countries is
summarized in "Dossier: Structural Adjustment," no. 111 The
Courier (September-October 1988).
131. See "Der Internationale Wahrungsfonds drängt Dar
es Salaam zur Advertung des Schilling," Handelsblatt,
August 16, 1988.
132. The medical fees are being indirectly introduced
by asking the patients to pay the so-called registration
fee. Currently this fee stands at Tshs. 20, but it is
likely to be raised with time.
133. In 1988-89 the school fees increased
tremendously. As of January 1, 1989, school fees for day
schools will be Tshs. 1500 (instead of Tshs. 750) and for
boarding schools will be Tshs. 3000 (instead of Tshs. 2000)
per pupil. See paragraph 91 of the budget speech by C. D.
Msuya, the minister for finance, economic affairs and
planning, presented to the National Assembly on June 16,
1988 and published by the Government Press, Dar es Salaam.
The former policy of the government on education is
analyzed in David R. Morrison, Education and Politics in
Africa: The Tanzanian Case.
134. On classes in Tanzania, see inter alia, Issa G.
Shivji, Silent Class Struggle (Dar es Salaam: Tanzania
Publishing House, 1973); Issa G. Shivji (ed.) The State
and the Working People in Tanzania; Issa G. Shivji, The
Class Struggles in Tanzania; and Paschal B. Mihyo,
Industrial Conflict and Change in Tanzania (Dar es Salaam:
Tanzania Publishing House, 1983).
135. On this incident, see Chris Peter and Sengondo
Mvungi, " The State and the Student Struggles," in Issa G.
Shivji (ed.) The State and the Working People in Tanzania,
p. 187.
136. See the Political Leaders' Pensions Act, 1981,
which is reproduced in the Special Supplement to the
Gazette of the United Republic of Tanzania, 27, Volume
LXII, July 3, 1981, p. 1.
137. See Specified State Leaders Retirement Benefits
Act, 1986 (Act Number 2 of 1986).
138. Section 3.
139. Section 13.

140. This issue was quite clear in the paper by Wolfgang Dourado titled "The Consolidation of the Union--A Basic Re-Appraisal," presented at the Tanganyika Law Society seminar on the NEC proposals for the amendment to the Union and Zanzibar Constitutions on July 28, 1983.

141. Frontline states are states which are neighbors of South Africa. Tanzania is one of them although it does not directly border South Africa. Maybe this is due to its immense contribution to the liberation struggle. On the role of these states, see Amadu Sesay, " The Roles of the Frontline States in Southern Africa," in Olajide Aluko and Timothy M. Shaw (eds.) Southern Africa in the 1980s (London: Allen and Unwin, 1983); and Amadu Sesay, et al The OAU after Twenty Years (Boulder, Colorado: Westview, 1984).

142. The role of the committee is discussed in Michael Wolfers, Politics in the Organization of African Unity (London: Methuen, 1976), Chapter 5.

143. This point is discussed at length above in connection with the right to own property.

144. Among the public enterprises established were the National Bank of Commerce (under Act No. 1 of 1967); State Trading Corporation (under Act No. 2 of 1967); National Agricultural Products Board (under Act No. 3 of 1967); and National Insurance Corporation (under Act No. 4 of 1967). See A. W. Bradley, "The Nationalizations of Companies in Tanzania," in P. A. Thomas (ed.) Private Enterprise and the East African Company (Dar es Salaam: Tanzania Publishing House, 1969); and Yash Ghai, "Law and Public Enterprise in Tanzania," in Law in the Political Economy of Public Enterprise (Uppsala: Scandinavian Institute of African Studies, 1977).

145. It is for this reason that the minister for finance, economic affairs and planning, Cleopa Msuya, has threatened that he is going to dismantle what he calls unprofitable state companies. See B. Lenga, "Planners at Economic Crossroads," no. 122 African Business (October 1988), p. 28.

146. See B. Lenga, "New Chapter for Tanzania Investors," no. 242, New African (November 1987), p. 62.

147. See C. Rabe, "In Tansania treiben pragmatische Politiker die wirtschaftliche Erholung voran: Dar es Salaam sucht neues Vertrauen," Handelsblatt, September 12, 1988; and Gunter Krabbe, "Mutiger Reformer," Frankfurter Allgemeine Zeitung, September 13, 1988.

148. This point was made by former president Nyerere in an interview when he was asked what Tanzania's greatest achievement was in the 20 years of independence. In reply, he said, "I think our greatest achievement is that we have consolidated ourselves as a nation." See Peter Enahoro, "Nyerere: The Private and Public," Africa Now, December 1983, p. 97. The same point is made in another context in Joel Samoff, "Single-Party Competitive Elections in Tanzania," in Fred Hayward (ed.), Elections in Independent Africa (Boulder, Colorado: Westview, 1987), p. 149.

149. See A. K. L. J. Mlimuka and P. J. A. M. Kabudi, "The State and the Party," in Issa G. Shivji (ed.), The State and the Working People in Tanzania.

150. B. Lenga, "Tanzania: Battle for the Economy," no. 253, New African (October 1988), p. 34. See also "Nyerere: CCM akzeptiert keinen Kapitalismus," Internationales Afrikaforum 29(3).

151. Cattle theft is a serious offense whose punishment on conviction is a 14-year jail term. See Section 268 of the Penal Code, Chapter 16 of the Laws of Tanzania. This section has to be read together with the relevant provisions of the Economic and Organized Crime Control Act, 1984 (Act No. 13 of 1984) as amended by the Economic and Organized Crime Control (Amendment) Act, 1987 (Act No. 12 of 1987) and the Stock Theft Ordinance, Chapter 422 of the Laws of Tanzania. The offense also falls under the Minimum Sentence Act, 1972.

152. On this form of traditional security force, see Ray Abrahams, "Sungu Sungu: Village Vigilante Groups in Tanzania," African Affairs 86, no. 343 (1987), p. 179.

153. This has moved to white-collar types of crimes and particularly affected is the National Bank of Commerce, whose chairman, Anon J. Nsekela, is reported to have said that "recently the Bank has witnessed a horrible spectra and crisis-size spate of thefts." See Brown Lenga, "Tanzania: Bank Robbers," no. 248, New African (May 1988), p. 18.

154. See M. Baker, L. Bassett, and A. Allington, The World Environment Handbook: A Directory of Natural Resources Management and Non-Governmental Environment Organizations in 145 Countries (New York: World Environment Center, 1985), p. 214.

155. On the pollution on the coast, see H. S. Kobola, and B. Mwaiseje, "Spotlight on Pollution," Sunday News (Tanzania), March 29, 1978; and C. M. Peter, "Report: Tanzania Marine Policy," Marine Policy: the International Journal of Ocean Affairs 7, no. 1 (1983), pp. 58-59.

156. See Sections 184, 185, and 186 of the Penal Code, Chapter 16 of the Laws of Tanzania.

157. See National Environment Management Act, 1983 (Act No. 19 of 1983).

158. Section 4 of Act No. 19 of 1983.

159. See National Land Use Planning Commission Act, 1984 (Act No. 3 of 1984).

160. See "Wastes Disposal Task Force Formed." Daily News (Tanzania), October 18, 1988.

161. Ibid.

Chapter 4
Enforcement Mechanism, Comparison, and Conclusion

Any law, national or international, is useful to the community only if it can be enforced. It does not serve any purpose to have a beautifully constructed and phrased legal instrument which cannot be put into action. In this chapter we examine the enforcement mechanism for the rights and freedoms provided for in the Banjul Charter and the Tanzanian Bill of Rights. This will indicate the usefulness of these two documents to the African people.

ENFORCEMENT MECHANISM UNDER THE BANJUL CHARTER

The Banjul Charter establishes a watch-dog to oversee respect for human rights on the continent in the form of the African Commission on Human and People's Rights.(1) This commission is to consist of eleven members from different African countries--African personalities of the highest reputation who are known for their morality, integrity, impartiality, and competence in human rights matters.(2) They shall be elected by the Assembly of Heads of State and Government.(3) The Assembly of Heads of State and Government elected the members of the first commission at the 23rd OAU summit, held in Addis Ababa, July 1987. The personalities elected are M. D. Mokama (Botswana), L. C. Mabanga Chipoya (Zambia), Alexis Gabou (Congo), Isaac Nguema (Gabon), Grace Ibingira (Uganda), Robert Eabesh Kisanga (Tanzania), Ali Mahmoud Hadmah (Libya), Ibrahim Badawi El-Sheikh (Egypt), Alione Blondin Baye (Mali), Youssoupha N'diaye (Senegal), and Sosurahata B. Semeye Janneh (Gambia). The members of the commission held its maiden session in Addis Ababa(4) in November 1987, where it elected the Gabonese lawyer Isaac Nguema as its first president. The position of vice-president went to Ibrahim Badawi El-Sheikh of Egypt.(5) The functions of the commission are enumerated in Article 45. They include promoting and ensuring the protection of human and people's rights.(6)
    The enforcement mechanism under the charter is through communications from member states. The charter provides that where a state has good reason to believe that another

is violating the provisions of the charter, then that
state shall first draw the attention of the state concerned
to the matter.(7)   The two states can then discuss the
matter amicably and settle it. However, if this fails, the
issue may be submitted to the Commission on Human and
People's Rights for investigation.   Alternatively, the
state which detected violation of the charter in another
may opt to refer the matter directly to the commission.(8)
     Having received a communication, the commission begins
its investigations.   It may ask the state alleged to have
violated the charter to provide it with all relevant
information.   When the commission is considering a
complaint against a state, that state may appear before
the commission and make written or oral representations.
(9) Having obtained all the information it requires, the
commission will attempt to remedy the situation through
communication with the state concerned; if this fails, the
matter plus recommendations will be submitted to the
Assembly of Heads of State and Government.(10)

ENFORCEMENT PROCEDURE UNDER THE TANZANIAN BILL OF RIGHTS

Enforcement of rights under the Tanzanian Bill of Rights
is straightforward.   Any individual whose fundamental
rights or freedoms have been violated can have recourse to
the law.(11)   The procedure for obtaining redress is to
file a suit in the High Court, which has jurisdiction as a
court of first instance.   A procedure for filing suits
related to fundamental rights will be provided in the law
to be enacted in the future by the parliament.(12) It was
hoped that this would be done before the Bill of Rights
came into force in March 1988 and that the state would
waive the cumbersome provisions in the 1967 Government
Proceedings Act, which require permission to be sought from
the government before it is sued.(13)   However, this was
not done and at present it is not clear what an aggrieved
person can actually do.
     Much will depend, in any event, on whether state
agencies will respect orders made by the courts of law on
human rights issues.   It is common knowledge that in
Tanzania the party and government functionaries and
especially the police do not respect court orders.(14)   If
this attitude continues, it will frustrate the whole
exercise of attempting to provide and guarantee fundamental
rights and freedoms to the people.

COMPARISON

The major differences between these two documents have
already been discussed. They relate to authorship and the
audiences to whom the documents are addressed. There are
differences also in terms of enforcement.   The Banjul
Charter, while well-framed in language and form, lacks
teeth when it comes to putting it into action.   There is
little that the African Commission on Human and People's
Rights can do other than communicate its findings to the
state alleged to be in violation of the charter.

Therefore, much depends on the aspect of good faith on the part of member states. This is a general problem in international law in which real enforcement depends on the principle of <u>pacts sunt servanda</u>--the principle of good faith. It is hoped that a rigorous publication of human rights violations in all forms will deter states as well.

The Tanzanian Bill of Rights, on the other hand, suffers from many aspects. To begin with, it is poorly drafted. Rights and freedoms are mixed such that some are placed where they do not belong, and there is also some lack of seriousness in stating certain rights and freedoms. On misplacement of rights, for example, torture, punishment, and humiliation are forbidden under Article 13 on equality before the law, whereas they ought to have been prohibited under the right to life in Article 14. Also, detention, arrest, remand, and repatriation, which are grouped under the right to life (Article 14), ought to have been mentioned under freedom of movement (Article 17). These are just random examples from the Bill of Rights which indicate poor draftsmanship. In addition, there has been an attempt to enact rights which the state does not intend to provide or guarantee. Freedom of association (Article 20) is a case in point. The Bill of Rights provides that everyone is free to establish or join a party with the objective of maintaining faith or interests. However, it is also clear that the ruling party has no intention of entertaining an opposition party. This seems to indicate a lack of seriousness on the part of the state in Tanzania. The same can be said with regard to freedom of movement (Article 17), which is surrounded with so many exceptions that it loses its meaning.

CONCLUSION

The two documents highlighted here are of extreme importance to the African people in general and particularly to Tanzanians. They stand as a testimony that the age when the fundamental rights of innocent people in Africa were trampled upon by colonial and postcolonial regimes has passed. They also re-echo the rights, freedoms, and dignity of all Africans. They also put into print what has always been promised by preceding regimes in Africa but never fulfilled.

On the other hand, they are a call for solidarity. Individuals are reminded that they are part of society and have duties to their fellow human beings. They therefore have to exercise their rights and freedoms in such a manner that they do not injure the interests of others.

There are other rights that can be realized only in a cooperative form. These include the right to development. The individual has to join others in society if these rights are to be realized. Therefore, the two documents, notwithstanding the deficiencies that may be found in them, must be seen as a beginning of a new era in Africa. That is an era of development in peace and dignity.

NOTES

1. Article 30.
2. Article 31.
3. Article 33.
4. For the term of each member of the Commission, see Appendix 3 which contains the list of members as released by the Permanent Delegation of the Organization of African Unity to the United Nations in Geneva.   We   extend our thanks to Professor Dr. Konrad Ginther of the Institut für Volkerrecht und Internationale Beziehungen der Karl-Franzens-Universität, Graz, Austria, for providing us with this important document.
5. See   "Menschenrechte   in   Africa,"   Frankfurter Allgemeine Zeitung, November 9, 1987 (no. 260), p. 7.
6. For the smooth carrying out of its functions, the commission adopted Rules of Procedure comprised of 120 articles on February 13, 1988. See "Rules of Procedure of the African Commission for Human and People's Rights," The Review: International Commission of Jurists 40 (June 1988), p. 26.
7. Article 47.
8. Article 49.
9. Article 51.
10. Articles 52 and 53.
11. Article 30(3).
12. Article 30(4).
13. The Government Proceedings Act, 1967 (Act No. 16 of 1967) has to be read together with Government Proceedings (Amendments) Act, 1974 (Act No. 49 of 1974). On an analysis of how this legislation is applied, see Legal Aid Committeè (Faculty of Law, University of Dar es Salaam), Essays on Law and Society, Chapter 3.
14. There are many documented incidences in which court orders have been ignored by authorities.   The most recent is reported from Mwanza Region in April 1987. There the Regional Police Commander, Triford Maji, refused to release property valued at shillings one million to Umoja wa kina Mama Ushonaji Co-operative Society despite a High Court Order made by Judge F. A. Munyera in October 1986. See "Mwanza Police Refusing Court Order?" Daily News (Tanzania), April 2, 1987.

Appendix I
The New Tanzanian Bill of Rights

The Constitution of the United Republic of Tanzania

SECTION THREE

RIGHTS AND OBLIGATIONS

Right to Equality

12. (1) All human beings are born free and all are equal.
  (2) Everyone deserves the respect of recognition and his life to be valued.
13. (1) All people are equal before the law, and have the right, without discrimination of any kind, to be protected and to be accorded equal justice before the law.
  (2) It is forbidden for any law enacted by an Authority in the United Republic to impose any condition which is of a discriminatory nature or which is obviously to one's disadvantage.
  (3) The rights of the people, the well-being and interests of everyone and the society will be protected and arbitrated by the courts and other organs of authority laid down by the law and in accordance with the law.
  (4) It is forbidden for anyone to be discriminated against by anyone or any authority which is exercising its powers under any law or in carrying out any duty or function of the Authority of the State or the Party and its instruments.
  (5) For the purposes of interpreting the conditions in this Article, the word "discrimination" means meeting the needs, rights or other requirements of different people based on their nationality, tribe, their origin, their political affiliation, color, religion or their lifestyles in such a way that certain people are made or considered inferior and subjected to restrictions or conditions of restrictions whereas other people are treated differently or are given opportunities or benefits that are outside the conditions or compulsory restrictions.
  (6) For the purposes of ensuring equality before the law, the Governing Authority will lay down appropriate guidelines or those that are in conformity with directions that—
    (a) When the rights and well-being of anyone need to be ascertained by a court of law or any other relevant organ of law or any other instrument, then that person will have the right to be given a chance to be listened to in full, also the right to appeal or to receive other legal consideration arising from the

decisions of the Court or of that other relevant instrument.

(b) It is forbidden for anyone who has been accused of a criminal offense to be considered guilty until it has been proved that the person is guilty of the offense.

(c) It is forbidden for anyone to be punished for any action which at the time of commission was not an offense under the law, and also that it is forbidden for a punishment to be given which is harsher than the punishment allowed at the time of the commission of the said offense.

(d) In order to maintain human justice and equality, human dignity will be protected in all areas and matters of investigation, and matters involving crime and in all other activities where an individual is under protective custody, or in ensuring the application of punishment.

(e) It is forbidden for a person to be tortured, to be punished unnaturally or to be given punishment that humiliates or degrades him.

The Right to Life

14. Everyone has the right to life and to receive from the society protection of his life, in accordance with the law.

15. (1) Everyone has the right to be free and to live as a free person.

(2) For the purposes of protecting the right of a person to be free and live in freedom, it will be forbidden for anyone to be arrested, jailed, remanded in custody, detained, forcibly repatriated or denied his freedom in any way, except only

(a) In accordance with the laid down guidelines under the law; or

(b) In carrying out judgement, order or punishment given by a court of law following the decision or conviction of a person for a criminal offence.

16. (1) Everyone deserves the respect and protection of his life, his individual right and that of his family and household, also respect and protection of his abode and his personal communication.

(2) For the purposes of maintaining individual rights in accordance with this Article, the governing Authority will lay down legal guidelines in respect of circumstances of how and to the extent in which private rights of a person and of his well-being, his property and his abode may be infringed upon without prejudice to the provisions of this Article.

17. (1) Every citizen of the United Republic has the right to go whenever he wishes in the United Republic, to live anywhere, to travel outside the country and to enter the country, and also the right not to be forced to emigrate or be expelled from the United Republic.

(2) Any legal action or any law whose intentions are-

(a) To diminish the freedom of a person to go whenever he wishes and to put him under guard or in

prison; or
        (b) To establish boundaries for use of freedom
of a person to go whenever he wishes so as-
            (i) To carry out judgement or order of a
        Court of law; or
            (ii) To force someone to complete first any
        obligation expected of him by other laws; or
            (iii) To protect national interests in
        general or to maintain certain special interests
        or   interests   of   a   certain section of society,
        such action will not be taken into consideration
        or that law will not be considered illegal or
        against this article.

The Right to Freedom of Conscience

18. (1) Without prejudice to the laws of the country,
everyone is free to express any opinion, to offer his
views, and to search for, to receive and to give
information and any ideas through any medium without
consideration to country boundaries, and is also free to
engage in personal communication without interference.
        (2) Every citizen has the right to be informed at all
times about different events taking place within the
country and around the world, events that are important to
his life and to the livelihood of the people, and also
about important social issues.
19. (1) Everyone is entitled to freedom of thought,
worship and choice on matters of religion.
        (2) Without prejudice to the laws applicable in the
United Republic, promotion of religion, worship and
evangelisation will be free and matters of personal
voluntary   choice,   and   activities pertaining to the
administration of religions will be outside the
jurisdiction of the State.
        (3) Whenever there is reference to "religion" in this
Article, it should be understood that its meaning also
includes religious denominations, and other references that
have identical meaning to the world, and such meanings will
be similarly interpreted.
(20) (1) Everyone deserves to be free, without prejudice
to the laws of the land, to interact voluntarily and
peacefully with other people, and to associate and
integrate with others, to offer his opinion publicly, and
on top of that, to establish or join a party or
organisations established with the objectives of
maintaining and promoting his faith or his interests or
other interests.
        (2) Without prejudice to the applicable laws of the
land, it is forbidden for anyone to be forced to join any
political party.
21. (1) Every citizen of the United Republic has the
right to participate in the affairs of governing the
country, either directly or through officials elected
voluntarily by the people in accordance with laid-down
guidelines and laws.
        (2) Every citizen has the right and freedom to
participate fully in the process of decision-making on

matters affecting him, his life and those affecting the nation.

The Right to Work

22.   (1)   Everyone has the right to work.
(2)   Every citizen deserves equal opportunity and rights under the conditions of equality, of holding any position of employment or activity under the authority of the state.
23.   (1)   Everyone without any discrimination, has the right to receive emoluments compatible with his work, and all the people who perform duties compatible with their qualifications will be paid according to their status and level of the position they hold.
(2)   Every working person deserves rightful emoluments.
24.   (1)   Without prejudice to the applicable laws of the land, everyone has the right to own property and the right to keep his property in accordance with the law.
(2)   Without prejudice to the provisions of subarticle (1), it is forbidden for anyone to be deprived of his property through nationalisation or through other means without recourse to law which lays down the procedure for fair compensation.
25.   (1)   Labour alone is the source of wealth of property in the community, is the foundation of prosperity for the people and the barometer for humanhood. Everyone has the obligation-
(a)   To engage willfully and honestly in legal productive labour; and
(b)   To maintain labour relations and endeavor to reach production goals on a personal basis and on a collective basis as required and as laid down by the law.
(2)   Without regard to sub-article (1), there will be no forced labour in the United Republic.
(3)   For the purposes of this article, and in this Constitution as a whole, let it be understood that no work will be considered forced, cruel or humiliating if that work, in accordance with the law, is-
(a)   Work required to be done as a result of judgement or court order;
(b)   Work that must be done by the armed forces of any kind in fulfilling their duties;
(c)   Work that anyone is required to do as a result of an emergency situation or any conflict that threatens the survival or prosperity of the society;
(d)   Any relief work that is part of-
(i)   Normal duties to ensure development of the society;
(ii) Compulsory nation building initiatives, in accordance with the law;
(iii) National efforts in harnessing the contribution of everyone in the work of developing the society and national economy and ensuring success in development.
26.   (1)   Everyone is expected to obey the Constitution and the laws of the United Republic.

(2) Everyone has the right, in complying with the guidelines established by law, to take legal actions to ensure the preservation of the Constitution and laws of the land.

27. (1) Everyone has the responsibility of conserving the natural resources of the United Republic, properly under the care of the State and all properties under the jurisdiction of the public, and also to respect the property of others.

(2) Everyone is expected to protect with care properties under care of the State, and of a collective nature, to combat all forms of destruction, and to participate in the economic development of the country in an orderly manner as if they are the future decision makers of the affairs of their nation.

28. (1) Every citizen has the responsibility of protecting, preserving and maintaining freedom, authority, land and national unity.

(2) Parliament may enact appropriate laws to enable the people to join the armed forces in the defense of the country.

(3) No one will have the right to sign an agreement accepting defeat in a war and to surrender the nation to the victor, or to acquiesce or recognise an act of invasion or division of the United Republic or of any section of the nation, and without prejudice to this Constitution and existing laws, no one shall have the right to stop the people of the United Republic from fighting a war against any enemy who may attack the country.

(4) Treason as interpreted by the law will be the highest form of crime against the United Republic.

General Conditions

29. (1) Everyone in the United Republic has the right to enjoy basic human rights and everyone has a duty to fulfill his obligation to the society, as explained in Articles 12 to 28 of this part of this chapter.

(2) Everyone in the Republic has the right to receive equal treatment under the laws of the United Republic.

(3) No citizen of the Republic will have rights, position of honour or special title based on lineage, origin or inheritance.

(4) It is forbidden by any law to confer rights, title or special honour to any citizen of the Republic based on lineage, origin or inheritance.

(5) For everyone to be able to enjoy rights and freedom as outlined in this Constitution, everyone has an obligation to act and to engage in his affairs in such a way that it will not interfere with the rights and freedoms of others, or interests of the public.

30. (1) Human rights and freedom whose foundation has been outlined in this Constitution will not be used by one person in a way that will result in interference or curtailment of rights and freedom of others or interests of the public.

(2) Let it be understood that conditions contained in this part of the Constitution, interpreting the rights,

freedom and human responsibilities do not illegalize in any way the established law or prevent any law from being enacted or any legal action being taken in accordance with that law, so as-

(a)   To ensure that justice and freedom of others or interests of the public are not violated by misuse of freedom and individual rights;

(b)   To ensure that security, safety of the society, peace of the community, good conduct in the community, community health, development programs in towns and villages, production and utilisation of minerals, or development and promotion of resources or any other interests aimed at developing the well-being of the public;

(c)   To ensure the implementation of judgement decisions or court order reached on any matter of civil or criminal nature;

(d)   To maintain the reputation, justice and freedom of the majority of the people or individual life of people involved in court decisions; to prevent conveyance of secret information; to maintain respect, authority and freedom of the court;

(e)   To impose restriction, administer and guard against the establishment, operation and matters of unions and private organisations in the country; or

(f)   To allow any other activity to take place, activity which will help develop and preserve the interests of the nation in general.

(3)   Anyone who claims that any condition in this part of the chapter or in any law relating to his rights or his obligations has been violated, is being violated or there are indications that it will be violated by anyone anywhere in the United Republic can file suit in the High Court.

(4)   Without prejudice to any other condition contained in this Constitution, the High Court will have the authority to hear for the first time and to offer judgement on any matter brought before the Court by referring to this Article; and the Authority of the State may enact a law so as-

(a)   To administer the procedure of filing suit in accordance with this Article;

(b)   To interpret the powers of the High Court in hearing the suit filed under this Article;

(c)   To ensure proper application of the powers of the High Court, protection and reinforcement of justice, freedom and obligations in accordance with this Constitution.

Exclusive Powers of the Authority of State

31.   (1)   Apart from the conditions contained in Article 30(2) any law enacted by Parliament will not be illegal just because it allows action to be taken during an emergency, or in case of ordinary time, against people believed to be engaged in actions that endanger or harm the security of the nation, actions which are in violation of Articles 14 and 15 of this Constitution.

(2)   It is forbidden for the actions mentioned in sub-

article (1) of this Article to be taken in accordance with
any law during an emergency or during ordinary time,
against anybody, except when such actions are necessary and
legal to deal with the situation during the period of the
state of emergency or during ordinary time to deal with the
situation caused by the person in question.
(3) Let it be understood that the conditions
contained in this Article will not sanction the deprivation
of one's rights to exist except due to death caused by acts
of war.
(4) For the purposes of this Article and the
following Articles in this Section, "during the period of
the state of emergency" means any period that the
Declaration of Emergency made by the President exercising
powers accorded him in Article 32, shall be in operation.
32. (1) Without prejudice to this Constitution or the law
enacted by Parliament for that purpose, the President may
declare a State of Emergency in the United Republic or in
any part of the Republic.
(2) The President can only declare a State of
Emergency when-
(a) The United Republic is in a state of war;
(b) There is a danger that the United Republic
is about to be invaded and ready to enter into a
state of war; or
(c) There is a threat to national peace or lack
of security for the people in the United Republic or
in any of its parts in such a way that necessitates
extraordinary measures to be taken to maintain peace
and security; or
(d) There is definite danger, of great
magnitude, to an extent that peace will be disrupted
and public safety will be endangered in the United
Republic or in any of its parts, a situation which can
only be contained by resorting to extra-ordinary
steps; or
(e) There is an impending danger or national
disaster that threatens the society or part of the
society in the United Republic; or
(f) There are other dangers that are obviously a
threat to the country.
(3) Whenever there is a State of Emergency in the
United Republic as a whole, or in Tanzania Zanzibar as a
whole or in Tanzania Mainland as a whole, the President
will serve a copy of that Declaration to the Secretary
General of the Party and to the Speaker of the National
Assembly who will deliberate and call a joint meeting of
the National Executive Committee and Parliament within a
period of 14 days in order to assess the situation and
decide whether to approve or disapprove the action which
will be adopted by a vote of not less than two-thirds of
the members, in support of the Declaration of a State of
Emergency made by the President.
(4) Parliament may enact a law laying down the
conditions in respect of the period and procedure that will
enable certain people charged with the implementation of
Government Authority in certain specific areas in the
United Republic to request the President to use his powers
given to him in this Article in respect of any of the areas

if there exists in those areas the situation mentioned in sub-sub-articles (c), (d) and (e) of sub-article (2) and that the situation does not spill over the boundaries of those areas; and also for the purpose of implementation of Government Authority during a State of Emergency.

(5) The Declaration of a State of Emergency made by the President in accordance with this Article will cease to be effective-

(a) Once it is abrogated by the President;

(b) When at the expiry of fourteen days after the Declaration is made no action has been taken as per sub-article (3) above;

(c) At the end of six months after the Declaration is made; except that a session of Parliament and the National Executive Committee can, before the expiry of six months extend periodically the duration of that Declaration up to a period of six more months based on a motion to be supported by not less than two-thirds of the votes of all members of that session;

(d) At any time when a joint session of Parliament and the National Executive Committee nullifies the Declaration by a motion to be supported by not less than two-thirds of the votes of all members.

(6) For the purpose of avoiding any ambiguities on the interpretation and implementation of the conditions in this Article, the conditions contained in the law enacted by Parliament and of any other law relating to the Declaration of a State of Emergency as mentioned in this Article, will only be applicable in the area of the United Republic where a State of Emergency has been declared.

Appendix II
African Charter on
Human and People's Rights

Preamble

The African States members of the Organization of
Africa Unity, parties to the present convention entitled
"African Charter on Human and People's Rights,"
Recalling Decision 115(XVI) of the Assembly of Heads
of State and Government at its Sixteenth Ordinary Session
held in Monrovia, Liberia, from July 17 to 10, 1979 on the
preparation of "a preliminary draft on an African Charter
on Human and People's Rights providing inter alia for the
establishment of bodies to promote and protect human and
people's rights";
Considering the Charter of the Organization of African
Unity, which stipulates that "freedom, equality, justice
and dignity are essential objectives for the achievement of
the legitimate aspirations of the African peoples";
Reaffirming the pledge they solemnly made in Article 2
of the said Charter to eradicate all forms of colonialism
from Africa, to coordinate and intensify their cooperation
and efforts to achieve a better life for the peoples of
Africa and to promote international cooperation having due
regard to the Charter of the United Nations and the
Universal Declaration of Human Rights;
Taking into consideration the virtues of their
historical tradition and the values of African civilization
which should inspire and characterize their reflection on
the concept of human and people's rights;
Recognizing on the one hand that fundamental human
rights stem from the attributes of human beings, which
justifies their national and international protection, and
on the other hand that the reality and respect of people's
rights should necessarily guarantee human rights;

---

*The Heads of State and Government of the Organisation of
African Unity at their 18th Assembly in Nairobi, June 24-
27, 1981, unanimously adopted the charter which had been
approved by the OAU Ministerial Conference in Banjul, the
Gambia, January 7-19, 1981, as OAU-Doc. CAB/LEG/67/3/Rev.5.

Considering that the enjoyment of rights and freedoms also implies the performance of duties on the part of everyone;

Convinced that it is henceforth essential to pay particular attention to the right to development and that civil and political rights cannot be disassociated from economic, social and cultural rights in their conception as well as universality and that the satisfaction of economic, social and cultural rights is a guarantee for the enjoyment of civil and political rights;

Conscious of their duty to achieve the total liberation of Africa, the peoples of which are still struggling for their dignity and genuine independence, and undertaking to eliminate colonialism, neo-colonialism, apartheid, zionism and to dismantle aggressive foreign military bases and all forms of discrimination, particularly those based on race, ethnic group, colour, sex, language, religion or political opinion;

Reaffirming their adherence to the principles of human and people's rights and freedoms contained in the declarations, conventions and other instruments adopted by the Organization of African Unity, the Movement of Non-Aligned Countries and the United Nations;

Firmly convinced of their duty to promote and protect human and people's rights and freedoms taking into account the importance traditionally attached to these rights and freedoms in Africa;

HAVE AGREED AS FOLLOWS:

PART I: Rights and Duties

Chapter I

Human and People's Rights

Article 1

The Member States of the Organization of African Unity parties to the present Charter shall recognize the rights, duties and freedoms enshrined in this Charter and shall undertake to adopt legislative and other measures to give effect to them.

Article 2

Every individual shall be entitled to the enjoyment of the rights and freedoms recognized and guaranteed in the present Charter without distinction of any kind such as race, ethnic group, colour, sex, language, religion, political or any other opinion, national and social origin, fortune, birth or other status.

Article 3

1.   Every individual shall be equal before the law.
2.   Every individual shall be entitled to equal protection of the law.

Article 4

Human beings are inviolable. Every human being shall

be entitled to respect for his life and the integrity of
his person.   No one may be arbitrarily deprived of this
right.

Article 5
Every individual shall have the right to the respect
of the dignity inherent in a human being and to the
recognition of his legal status. All forms of exploitation
and degradation of man particularly slavery, slave trade,
torture, cruel, inhuman or degrading punishment and
treatment shall be prohibited.

Article 6
Every individual shall have the right to liberty and
to the security of his person. No one may be deprived of
his freedom except for reasons and conditions previously
laid down by law, in particular, no one may be arbitrarily
arrested or detained.

Article 7
1.   Every individual shall have the right to have his
cause heard.   This comprises:
(a) The right to an appeal to competent national
organs against acts of violating his fundamental rights as
recognized and guaranteed by conventions, laws, regulations
and customs in force;
(b) The right to be presumed innocent until proved
guilty by a competent court or tribunal;
(c) The right to defence, including the right to be
defended by counsel of his choice;
(d) The right to be tried within a reasonable time by
an impartial court or tribunal.
2.   No one may be condemned for an act or omission which
did not constitute a legally punishable offence at the time
it was committed.   No penalty may be inflicted for an
offence for which no provision was made at the time it was
committed.   Punishment is personal and can be imposed only
on the offender.

Article 8
Freedom of conscience, the profession and free
practice of religion shall be guaranteed. No one may,
subject to law and order, be submitted to measures
restricting the exercise of these freedoms.

Article 9
1.   Every individual shall have the right to receive
information.
2.   Every individual shall have the right to express and
disseminate his opinions within the law.

Article 10
1.   Every individual shall have the right to free
association provided that he abides by the law.
2.   Subject to the obligation of solidarity provided for
in Article 29 no one may be compelled to join an
association.

Article 11

Every individual shall have the right to assemble
freely with others. The exercise of this right shall be
subject only to necessary restrictions provided for by law
in particular those enacted in the interest of national
security, the safety, health, ethics and rights and
freedoms of others.
1.   Every individual shall have the right to freedom of
movement and residence within the borders of a State
provided he abides by the law.
2.   Every individual shall have the right to leave any
country including his own, and to return to his country.
This right may only be subject to restrictions, provided
for by law for the protection of national security, law and
order, public health or morality.
3.   Every individual shall have the right, when
persecuted, to seek and obtain asylum in other countries in
accordance with the laws of those countries and
international conventions.
4.   A non-national legally admitted in a territory of a
State Party to the present Charter, may only be expelled
from it by virtue of a decision taken in accordance with
the law.
5.   The mass expulsion of non-nationals shall be
prohibited. Mass expulsion shall be that which is aimed at
national, racial, ethnic or religious groups.

Article 13
1.   Every citizen shall have the right to participate
freely in the government of his country, either directly or
through freely chosen representatives in accordance with
the provisions of the law.
2.   Every citizen shall have the right of equal access to
the public service of his country.
3.   Every individual shall have the right of access to
public property and services in strict equality of all
persons before the law.

Article 14
The right to property shall be guaranteed. It may
only be encroached upon in the interest of public need or
in the general interest of the community and in accordance
with the provisions of appropriate laws.

Article 15
Every individual shall have the right to work under
equitable and satisfactory conditions, and shall receive
equal pay for equal work.

Article 16
1.   Every individual shall have the right to enjoy the
best attainable state of physical and mental health.
2.   State Parties to the present Charter shall take the
necessary measures to protect the health of their people
and to ensure that they receive medical attention when they
are sick.

Article 17
1.   Every individual shall have the right to education.
2.   Every individual may freely take part in the cultural

life of his community.
3.   The promotion and protection of morals and traditional
values recognized by the community shall be the duty of the
State.

Article 18
1.   The family shall be the natural unit and basis of
society.   It shall   be protected   by the   State which shall
take care of its physical and moral health.
2.   The State shall have the duty to assist the family
which is the custodian of morals and traditional values
recognized by the community.
3.   The State shall ensure the elimination of every
discrimination against women and also ensure the protection
of the rights of the woman and child as stipulated in
international declarations and conventions.
4.   The aged and the disabled shall also have the right to
special measures of protection in keeping with their
physical or moral needs.

Article 19
     All peoples shall be equal; they shall enjoy the same
respect and shall have the same rights.   Nothing shall
justify the domination of a people by another.

Article 20
1.   All peoples shall have the right to existence.   They
shall have the unquestionable and inalienable right to
self-determination.   They shall freely determine their
political status and shall pursue their economic and social
development according to the policy they have freely
chosen.
2.   Colonized or oppressed peoples shall have the right to
free themselves from the bonds of domination by resorting
to any means recognized by the international community.
3.   All peoples shall have the right to the assistance of
the State Parties to the present Charter in their
liberation struggle against foreign domination, be it
political, economic or cultural.

Article 21
1.   All peoples shall freely dispose of their wealth and
natural resources.   This right shall be exercised in the
exclusive interest of the people.   In no case shall a
people be deprived of it.
2.   In case of spoliation the dispossessed people shall
have the right to the lawful recovery of its property as
well as to an adequate compensation.
3.   The free disposal of wealth and natural resources
shall be exercised without prejudice to the obligation of
promoting international economic cooperation based on
mutual respect, equitable exchange and the principles of
international law.
4.   States Parties to the present Charter shall
individually and collectively exercise the right to free
disposal of their wealth and natural resources with a view
to strengthening African unity and solidarity.
5.   States Parties to the present Charter shall undertake
to eliminate all forms of foreign economic exploitation

particularly that practised by international monopolies so
as to enable their peoples to fully benefit from the
advantages derived from their national resources.

Article 22
1.   All peoples shall have the right to their economic,
social and cultural development with due regard to their
freedom and identity and in the equal enjoyment of the
common heritage of mankind.
2.   States   shall   have   the   duty,   individually or
collectively, to ensure the exercise of the right to
development.

Article 23
1.   All peoples shall have the right to national and
international peace and security.   The principles of
solidarity and friendly relations implicitly affirmed by
the Charter of the United Nations and reaffirmed by that of
the Organization of African Unity shall govern relations
between States.
2.   For the purpose of strengthening peace, solidarity and
friendly relations, States Parties to the present Charter
shall ensure that:
     (a) any individual enjoying the right of asylum under
Article 12 of the present Charter shall not engage in
subversive activities against his country of origin or any
other State party to the present Charter;
     (b) their territories shall not be used as bases for
subversive or terrorist activities against the people of
any other State party to the present Charter.

Article 24
     All peoples shall have the right to a general
satisfactory environment favourable to their development.

Article 25
     States Parties to the present Charter shall have the
duty to promote and ensure through teaching, education and
publication, the respect of the rights and freedoms
contained in the present Charter and to see to it that
these freedoms and rights as well as corresponding
obligations and duties are understood.

Article 26
     States Parties to the present Charter shall have the
duty to guarantee the independence of the Courts and shall
allow the establishment and improvement of appropriate
national institutions entrusted with the promotion and
protection of the rights and freedoms guaranteed by the
present Charter.

Chapter II

Duties

Article 27
1.   Every individual shall have duties towards his family
and society, the state and other legally recognized

communities and the international community.
2.   The rights   and freedoms   of each   individual shall be
exercised   with   due   regard   to   the   rights   of   others,
collective security, morality and common interest.

Article 28

Every individual   shall have   the duty   to respect and
consider his, fellow beings   without discrimination, and to
maintain relations   aimed   at   promoting,   safeguarding and
reinforcing mutual respect and tolerance.

Article 29

The individual shall also have the duty:
1.   To preserve   the harmonious   development of the family
and to work for the cohesion and respect of the   family; to
respect his   parents at all times, to maintain them in case
of need.
2.   To   serve   his   national   community   by   placing   his
physical and intellectual abilities at its service;
3.   Not   to   compromise   the   security   of the State whose
national or resident he is;
4.   To   preserve   and   strengthen   social   and   national
solidarity, particularly when the latter is threatened;
5.   To preserve and strengthen   the national independence
and   the   territorial   integrity   of   his   country   and   to
contribute to its defense in accordance with the law.
6.   To work   to the   best of his abilities and competence,
and to pay taxes imposed by   law   in   the   interest   of the
society;
7.   To preserve   and strengthen   positive African cultural
values in his relations with other members of   the society,
in the   spirit of tolerance, dialogue and consultation and,
in general, to contribute to   the   promotion   of   the moral
well-being of society;
8.   To   contribute   to   the   best of his abilities, at all
times and at all levels, to   the promotion   and achievement
of African unity.

PART II: Measures of Safeguard

Chapter I

Establishment   and   Organization   of   the   African
Commission on Human and People's Rights

Article 30

An African Commission on   Human   and   People's Rights,
hereinafter called   "the Commission,"   shall be established
within the Organization of African Unity   to promote human
and people's rights and ensure their protection in Africa.

Article 31

1.   The Commission   shall consist of eleven members chosen
from   amongst   African   personalities   of   the   highest
reputation,   known   for   their   high   morality,   integrity,
impartiality   and   competence   in   matters   of   human   and
people's   rights;   particular   consideration being given to
persons having legal experience.

2.   The members of the Commission shall serve in their
personal capacity.

Article 32
The Commission shall not include more than one
national of the same State.

Article 33
The members of the Commission shall be elected by
secret ballot by the Assembly of Heads of State and
Government, from a list of persons nominated by the States
parties to the present charter.

Article 34
Each State party to the present Charter may not
nominate more than two candidates. The candidates must
have the nationality of one of the States parties to the
present Charter. When two candidates are nominated by a
State, one of them may not be a national of that State.

Article 35
1.   The Secretary General of the Organization of African
Unity shall invite States parties to the present Charter at
least four months before the elections to nominate
candidates;
2.   The Secretary General of the Organization of African
Unity shall make an alphabetical list of the persons thus
nominated and communicate it to the Heads of State and
Government at least one month before the elections.

Article 36
The members of the Commission shall be elected for a
six-year period and shall be eligible for reelection.
However, the term of office of four of the members elected
at the first election shall terminate after two years and
the term of office of three others, at the end of four
years.

Article 37
Immediately after the first election, the Chairman of
the Assembly of Heads of State and Government of the
Organization of African Unity shall draw lots to decide the
names of those members referred to in Article 36.

Article 38
After their election, the members of the Commission
shall make a solemn declaration to discharge their duties
impartially and faithfully.

Article 39
1.   In case of death or resignation of a member of the
Commission, the Chairman of the Commission shall
immediately inform the Secretary General of the
Organization of African Unity, who shall declare the seat
vacant from the date of death or from the date on which the
resignation takes effect.
2.   If, in the unanimous opinion of other members of the
Commission, a member has stopped discharging his duties for
any reason other than a temporary absence, the Chairman of

the Commission shall inform the Secretary General of the
Organization of African Unity who shall then declare the
seat vacant.
3. In each of the cases anticipated above, the Assembly
of Heads of State and Government shall replace the member
whose seat became vacant for the remaining period of his
term unless the period is less than six months.

Article 40
Every member of the Commission shall be in office
until the date his successor assumes office.

Article 41
The Secretary General of the Organization of African
Unity shall appoint the Secretary of the Commission. He
shall also provide the staff and services necessary for the
effective discharge of the duties of the Commission. The
Organization of African Unity shall bear the costs of the
staff and services.

Article 42
1. The Commission shall elect its Chairman and Vice
Chairman for a two-year period. They shall be eligible for
reelection.
2. The Commission shall lay down its rules of procedure.
3. Seven members shall form the quorum.
4. In case of an equality of votes, the Chairman shall
have a casting vote.
5. The Secretary General may attend the meetings of the
Commission. He shall neither participate in deliberations
nor shall he be entitled to vote. The Chairman of the
Commission may, however, invite him to speak.

Article 43
In discharging their duties, members of the Commission
shall enjoy diplomatic privileges and immunities provided
for in the General Convention on the Privileges and
Immunities of the Organization of African Unity.

Article 44
Provision shall be made for the emoluments and
allowances of the members of the Commission in the Regular
budget of the Organization of African Unity.

Chapter II

Mandate of the Commission

The functions of the Commission shall be:
1. To promote Human and People's Rights and in
particular:
    (a) To collect documents, undertake studies and
researches on African problems in the field of human and
people's rights, organize seminars, symposia and
conferences, disseminate information, encourage national
and local institutions concerned with human and people's
rights, and should the case arise, give its views or make
recommendations to Governments;

(b) To formulate and lay down, principles and rules aimed at solving legal problems relating to human and people's rights and fundamental freedoms upon which African Governments may base their legislation;

(c) Cooperate with other African and international institutions concerned with the promotion and protection of human and people's rights.

2. Ensure the protection of human and people's rights under conditions laid down by the present Charter.

3. Interpret all the provisions of the present Charter at the request of a State Party, an institution of the OAU or an African organization recognized by the OAU.

4. Perform any other tasks which may be entrusted to it by the Assembly of Heads of State and Government.

Chapter III

Procedure of the Commission

Article 46

The Commission may resort to any appropriate method of investigation; it may hear from the Secretary General of the Organization of African Unity or any other person capable of enlightening it.

Communication from States

Article 47

If a State Party to the present Charter has good reason to believe that another State Party to the Charter has violated the provisions of the Charter, it may draw, by written communication, the attention of that State to the matter. This communication shall also be addressed to the Secretary General of the OAU and to the Chairman of the Commission. Within three months of the receipt of the communication, the State to which the communication is addressed shall give the enquiring State written explanation of statement elucidating the matter. This should include as much as possible relevant information relating to the laws and rules of procedure applied and applicable, and the redress already given or course of action available.

Article 48

If within three months from the date on which the original communication is received by the State to which it is addressed, the issue is not settled to the satisfaction of the two States involved through bilateral negotiation or by any other peaceful procedure, either State shall have the right to submit the matter to the Commission through the Chairman and shall notify the other States involved.

Article 49

Notwithstanding the provisions of Article 47, if a State Party to the present Charter considers that another State Party has violated the provisions of the Charter, it may refer the matter directly to the Commission by addressing a communication to the Chairman, to the

Secretary General of the Organization of African Unity and
the State concerned.

Article 50
The Commission can only deal with a matter submitted
to it after making sure that all local remedies, if they
exist, have been exhausted, unless it is obvious to the
Commission that the procedure of achieving these remedies
would be unduly prolonged.

Article 51
1.   The Commission may ask the States concerned to provide
it with all relevant information.
2.   When the Commission is considering the matter, States
concerned may be represented before it and submit written
or oral representations.

Article 52
After having obtained from the States concerned and
from other sources all the information it deems necessary
and after having tried all appropriate means to reach an
amicable solution based on the respect of Human and
People's Rights, the Commission shall prepare, within a
reasonable period of time from the notification referred to
in Article 48, a report stating the facts and its findings.
This report shall be sent to the States concerned and
communicated to the Assembly of Heads of State and
Government.

Article 53
While transmitting its report, the Commission may make
to the Assembly of Heads of State and Government such
recommendations as it deems useful.

Article 54
The Commission shall submit to each Ordinary Session
of the Assembly of Heads of State and Government a report
on its activities.

Other Communications

Article 55
1.   Before each Session, the Secretary of the Commission
shall make a list of the communications other than those of
State Parties to the present Charter and transmit them to
the members of the Commission, who shall indicate which
communications should be considered by the Commission.
2.   A communication shall be considered by the Commission
if a simple majority of its members so decide.

Article 56
Communications relating to human and people's rights
referred to in Article 55 received by the Commission, shall
be considered if they:
1.   Indicate their authors even if the latter request
anonymity.
2.   Are compatible with the Charter of the Organization of
African Unity or with the present Charter.

3.   Are not written in disparaging or insulting language
directed against the State concerned and its institutions
or to the Organization of African Unity.
4.   Are not based exclusively on news disseminated through
the mass media.
5.   Are sent after exhausting local remedies, if any,
unless it is obvious that this procedure is unduly
prolonged.
6.   Are submitted within a reasonable period from the time
local remedies are exhausted or from the date the
Commission is seized of the matter, and
7.   Do not deal with cases which have been settled by
these States involved in accordance with the principles of
the Charter of the United Nations, or the Charter of the
Organization of African Unity or the provisions of the
present Charter.

Article 57
    Prior   to   any   substantive   consideration,   all
communications shall be brought to the knowledge of the
State concerned by the Chairman of the Commission.

Article 58
1.   When it appears after deliberations of the Commission
that one or more communications apparently relate to
special cases revealing the existence of a series of
serious or massive violations of human and people's rights,
the Commission shall draw the attention of the Assembly of
Heads of State and Government to these special cases.
2.   The Assembly of Heads of State and Government may then
request the Commission to undertake an in-depth study of
these cases and make a factual report, accompanied by its
finding and recommendations.
3.   A case of emergency duly noticed by the Commission
shall be submitted by the latter to the Chairman of the
Assembly of Heads of State and Government who may request
an in-depth study.

Article 59
1.   All measures taken within the provisions of the
present Chapter shall remain confidential until such a time
as the Assembly of Heads of State and Government shall
otherwise decide.
2.   However, the report shall be published by the Chairman
of the Commission upon the decision of the Assembly of
Heads of State and Government.
3.   The report on the activities of the Commission shall
be published by its Chairman after it has been considered
by the Assembly of Heads of State and Government.

Chapter IV

Applicable Principles

Article 60
    The   Commission   shall   draw   inspiration   from
international   law   on   human   and   people's   rights,
particularly from   the   provisions   of   various   African

instruments on human and people's rights, the Charter of
the United Nations, the Charter of the Organization of
African Unity, the Universal Declaration of Human Rights,
other instruments adopted by the United Nations and by
African countries in the field of human and people's rights
as well as from the provisions of various instruments
adopted within the Specialized Agencies of the United
Nations of which the parties to the present Charter are
members.

Article 61
The Commission shall also take into consideration, as
subsidiary measures to determine the principles of law,
other general or special international conventions, laying
down rules expressly recognized by member states of the
Organization of African Unity, African practices consistent
with international norms on human and people's rights,
customs generally accepted as law, general principles of
law recognized by African states as well as legal
precedents and doctrine.

Article 62
Each State Party shall undertake to submit every two
years, from the date the present Charter comes into force,
a report on the legislative or other measures taken with a
view to giving effect to the rights and freedoms recognized
and guaranteed by the present Charter.

Article 63
1. The present Charter shall be open to signature,
ratification or adherence of the member states of the
Organization of African Unity.
2. The instrument of ratification or adherence to the
present Charter shall be deposited with the Secretary
General of the Organization of African Unity.
3. The present Charter shall come into force three months
after reception by the Secretary General of the instruments
of ratification of adherence by a simple majority of the
member states of the Organization of African Unity.

PART III: GENERAL PROVISIONS

Article 64
1. After the coming into force of the present Charter,
members of the Commission shall be elected in accordance
with the relevant Articles of the present Charter.
2. The Secretary General of the Organization of African
Unity shall convene the first meeting of the Commission at
the Headquarters of the Organization within three months of
the constitution of the Commission. Thereafter, the
Commission shall be convened by its Chairman whenever
necessary but at least once a year.

Article 65
For each of the States that will ratify or adhere to
the present Charter after its coming into force, the
charter shall take effect three months after the date of
the deposit by that State of its instrument of ratification

or adherence.

Article 66
Special protocols or agreements may, if necessary, supplement the provisions of the present Charter.

Article 67
The Secretary General of the Organization of African Unity shall inform member states of the Organization of the deposit of each instrument of ratification or adherence.

Article 68
The present Charter may be amended if a State Party makes a written request to that effect to the Secretary General of the Organization of African Unity. The Assembly of Heads of State and Government may only consider the draft amendment after all the States Parties have been duly informed of it and the Commission has given its opinion on it at the request of the sponsoring State. The amendment shall be approved by a simple majority of the States Parties. It shall come in to force for each State which has accepted it in accordance with its constitutional procedure three months after the Secretary General has received notice of the acceptance.

Appendix III
Composition of the African Commission on Human and People's Rights

One of the major decisions taken by the 23rd OAU Summit held in Addis Ababa July 27-29, 1987, was the establishment of an eleven-member African Commission on Human and People's Rights.

The following were selected by the Heads of State and Government:

M. D. McKama, Botswana	for 6 years
L. C. Mubanga Chipoya, Zambia	" 4 years
Alexis Gabou, Congo	" 6 years
Isaac Nguema, Gabon	" 2 years
Grace Ibingira, Uganda	" 4 years
Robert Eabesh Kisanga, Tanzania	" 4 years
Ali Mahmoud Hadmah, Libya	" 4 years
Ibrahim Badawi El-Sheikh, Egypt	" 2 years
Alioune Blondin Beye, Mali	" 2 years
Youssoupha N'Diaye, Senegal	" 6 years
Sourahata B. Semege Janneh, Gambia	" 2 years

The basic functions of the commission are to promote human and people's rights and ensure their protection in Africa.

The African Charter on Human and People's Rights entered into force in October 1986 after the OAU Secretary-General received the instruments of ratification of a simple majority of the organization's membership.

Appendix IV
The Universal Declaration of Human Rights

Adopted and proclaimed by General Assembly Resolution 217A
(111) of 10 December 1948.

Preamble

Whereas recognition of the inherent dignity and of the
equal and inalienable rights of all members of the human
family is the foundation of freedom, justice and peace in
the world,

Whereas disregard and contempt for human rights have
resulted in barbarous acts which have outraged the
conscience of mankind, and the advent of a world in which
human beings shall enjoy freedom of speech and belief and
freedom from fear and want has been proclaimed as the
highest aspiration of the common people,

Whereas it is essential, if man is not to be compelled
to have recourse, as a last resort, to rebellion against
tyranny and oppression, that human rights should be
protected by the rule of law,

Whereas it is essential to promote the development of
friendly relations between nations,

Whereas the peoples of the United Nations have in the
Charter reaffirmed their faith in fundamental human rights,
in the dignity and worth of the human person and in the
equal rights of men and women and have determined to
promote social progress and better standards of life in
larger freedom,

Whereas Member States have pledged themselves to
achieve, in cooperation with the United Nations, the
promotion of universal respect for and observance of human
rights and fundamental freedoms,

Whereas a common understanding of these rights and
freedoms is of the greatest importance for the full
realization of this pledge,

Now, therefore,

The General Assembly

Proclaims this Universal Declaration of Human Rights
as a common standard of achievement for all peoples and all
nations, to the end that every individual and every organ
of society, keeping this Declaration constantly in mind,

shall strive by teaching and education to promote respect
for these   rights and freedoms and by progressive measures,
national and international, to   secure their   universal and
effective   recognition   and observance,   both among the
peoples of Member States themselves and among the peoples
of territories under this jurisdiction.

Article 1
All human beings are born free and equal in dignity
and rights. They are endowed with reason and conscience
and   should   act   towards   one   another   in   a   spirit   of
brotherhood.

Article 2
Everyone is entitled to all the   rights and freedoms
set forth in this Declaration, without distinction of any
kind,   such   as   race,   colour,   sex,   language,   religion,
political   or   other   opinion,   national   or social origin,
property, birth or other status.
Furthermore, no distinction shall be made on the basis
of the political, jurisdictional or international status of
the country or territory to which a person belongs, whether
it be   independent, trust, non-self-governing or under any
other limitation of sovereignty.

Article 3
Everyone has the right to life,   liberty and security
of person.

Article 4
No one shall be held in slavery or servitude; slavery
and the slave trade shall be prohibited in all their forms.

Article 5
No one shall be subjected to torture or to cruel,
inhuman or degrading treatment or punishment.

Article 6
Everyone has the right to recognition everywhere as a
person before the law.

Article 7
All are equal before the law and are entitled without
any discrimination to equal protection of the law. All are
entitled to equal protection against any discrimination in
violation of this Declaration and against any incitement to
such discrimination.

Article 8
Everyone has the right to an effective remedy by the
competent national   tribunals   for   acts violating the
fundamental rights granted him by the constitution or by
law.

Article 9
No one   shall be subjected to arbitrary arrest,
detention or exile.

Article 10

Everyone is entitled in full equality to a fair and public hearing by an independent and impartial tribunal, in the determination of his rights and obligations and of any criminal charge against him.

Article 11

1.   Everyone charged with a penal offence has the right to be presumed innocent until proved guilty according to law in a public trial at which he has had all the guarantees necessary for his defence.

2.   No one shall be held guilty of any penal offence on account of any act or omission which did not constitute a penal offence, under national or international law, at the time when it was committed. Nor shall a heavier penalty be imposed than the one that was applicable at the time the penal offence was committed.

Article 12

No one shall be subjected to arbitrary interference with his privacy, family, home or correspondence, nor to attacks upon his honour and reputation. Everyone has the right to the protection of the law against such interference or attacks.

Article 13

1.   Everyone has the right to freedom of movement and residence within the borders of each state.

2.   Everyone has the right to leave any country, including his own, and to return to his country.

Article 14

1.   Everyone has the right to seek and to enjoy in other countries asylum from persecution.

2.   This right may not be invoked in the case of prosecutions genuinely arising from non-political crimes or from acts contrary to the purposes and principles of the United Nations.

Article 15

1.   Everyone has the right to nationality.

2.   No one shall be arbitrarily deprived of his nationality nor denied the right to change his nationality.

Article 16

1.   Men and women of full age, without any limitation due to race, nationality, or religion, have the right to marry and to found a family. They are entitled to equal rights as to marriage, during marriage and at its dissolution.

2.   Marriage shall be entered into only with the free and full consent of the intending spouses.

3.   The family is the natural and fundamental group unit of society and is entitled to protection by society and the State.

Article 17

1.   Everyone has the right to own property alone as well as in association with others.

2.   No one shall be arbitrarily deprived of his property.

Article 18
Everyone has the right to freedom of thought, conscience and religion; this right includes freedom to change his religion or belief, and freedom, either alone or in community with others and in public or private, to manifest his religion or belief in teaching, practice, worship and observance.

Article 19
Everyone has the right to freedom of opinion and expression; this right includes freedom to hold opinions without interference and to seek, receive and impart information and ideas through any media and regardless of frontiers.

Article 20
1.   Everyone has the right to freedom of peaceful assembly and association.
2.   No one may be compelled to belong to any association.

Article 21
1.   Everyone has the right to take part in the government of his country, directly or through freely chosen representatives.
2.   Everyone has the right of equal access to public service in this country.
3.   The will of the people shall be the basis of the authority of government; this will shall be expressed in periodic and genuine elections which shall be by universal and equal suffrage and shall be held by secret vote or by equivalent free voting procedures.

Article 22
Everyone, as a member of society, has the right to social security and is entitled to realization, through national effort and international cooperation and in accordance with the organization and resources of each State, of the economic, social and cultural rights indispensable for his dignity and the free development of his personality.

Article 23
1.   Everyone has the right to work, to free choice of employment, to just and favourable conditions of work and to protection against unemployment.
2.   Everyone, without any discrimination, has the right to equal pay for equal work.
3.   Everyone who works has the right to just and favorable remuneration ensuring for himself and his family an existence worthy of human dignity, and supplemented, if necessary, by other means of social protection.
4.   Everyone has the right to form and to join trade unions for the protection of his interests.

Article 24
Everyone has the right to rest and leisure, including reasonable limitation of working hours and periodic holidays with pay.

Article 25

1.   Everyone has the right to a standard of living
adequate for the health and well-being of himself and of
his family, including food, clothing, housing and medical
care and necessary social services, and the right to
security in the event of unemployment, sickness,
disability, widowhood, old age or other lack of livelihood
in circumstances beyond his control.
2.   Motherhood and childhood are entitled to special care
and assistance. All children, whether born in or out of
wedlock, shall enjoy the same social protection.

Article 26

1.   Everyone has the right to education. Education shall
be free, at least in the elementary and fundamental stages.
Elementary education shall be compulsory. Technical and
professional education shall be made generally available
and higher education shall be equally accessible to all on
the basis of merit.
2.   Education shall be directed to the full development of
the human personality and to the strengthening of respect
for human rights and fundamental freedoms.   It shall
promote understanding, tolerance and friendship among all
nations, racial or religious groups, and shall further the
activities of the United Nations for the maintenance of
peace.
3.   Parents have a prior right to choose the kind of
education that shall be given to their children.

Article 27

1.   Everyone has the right freely to participate in the
cultural life of the community, to enjoy the arts and to
share in scientific advancement and its benefits.
2.   Everyone has the right to the protection of the moral
and material interests resulting from any scientific,
literary or artistic production of which he is the author.

Article 28

Everyone is entitled to a social and international
order in which the rights and freedoms set forth in the
Declaration can be fully realized.

Article 29

1.   Everyone has duties to the community in which alone
the free and full development of his personality is
possible.
2.   In the exercise of his rights and freedoms, everyone
shall be subject only to such limitations as are determined
by law solely for the purposes of securing due recognition
and respect for the rights and freedoms of others and of
meeting the just requirements of morality, public order and
the general welfare in a democratic society.
3.   These rights and freedoms may in no case be exercised
contrary to the purposes and principles of the United
Nations.

Article 30

Nothing in this Declaration may be interpreted as
implying for any State, group or person any right to engage

in any activity or to perform any act aimed at the destruction of any of the rights and freedoms set forth herein.

Text produced from: United Nations – Human Rights: A Compilation of International Instruments– ST/HR/1/REV.2 (1983), pp. 1/3.

Appendix V
Summary of Rights, Freedoms, Duties, and Obligations in (1) the Tanzanian Bill of Rights (1984), (2) the African Charter on Human and People's Rights (1981), and (3) the Universal Declaration on Human Rights (1948)

Summary of Rights, Freedoms, Duties, and Obligations in
(1) the Tanzanian Bill of Rights (1984), (2) the African
Charter on Human and People's Rights (1981), and (3) the
Universal Declaration of Human Rights (1948)

Right, Freedom, Duty or Obligation	Tanzanian Bill of Rights (Article)	African Charter (Article)	Universal Declaration (Article)
Equality of all	12	2	1
Equality before the law	13	3(1)	7
Right to Life	14	4	3
Right to Liberty & Security of Person	15	6	3
Right to Respect & Protection of Life	16	4	3
Freedom of Movement	17	12	13
Freedom of Expression	18	9(2)	19
Freedom of Worship	19	8	18
Freedom of Association	20	10(1)	20
Right to Participate in National Affairs	21	13(1)	21
Right to Work	22	15	23(1)
Right to Just Emoluments	23	15	23(2)
Right to Own Property	24	14	17
Right to Education	11*	17(1)	26
Obligation to Work	25	29(6)	29
Obligation to Obey Laws of the Country	26	28(1)	29**
Obligation to Protect Public Property	27	29(5)	29**
Obligation to Protect & Preserve National Security	28	29(3)	29**

*Article 11 in the Tanzanian Constitution, which provides
for the right to education together with other rights such
as the right to receive assistance from society at old age
or when sick and disabled, is actually outside the purview
of the Bill of Rights, which begins with Article 12.

**The Universal Declaration of Human Rights, 1948, does not
emphasize obligations of the individual.

Appendix VI
Cases and Statutes

Ally Linus and Eleven Others vs. Tanzania Harbours Authority, High Court of Tanzania at Dar es Salaam, Miscellaneous Civil Cause No. 5 of 1980.

Amri Juma and Fifteen Others vs. Tanzania Harbours Authority, High Court of Tanzania at Dar es Salaam, Miscellaneous Civil Cause No. 37 of 1980.

Attorney-General vs. Lesinoi Ndenai and Two Others, Court of Appeal of Tanzania at Arusha, Criminal Appeal No. 52 of 1979 and Criminal Appeal No. 53 of 1979.

Banco Nacional de Cuba vs. Sabbatino (1964), 376 US 398.

Feliya Kachasu (an infant by her father and next friend Paul Kachasu) vs. Attorney-General, High Court of Zambia at Lusaka, Civil Jurisdiction Selected Judgments of Zambia No. 10 of 1969 (1967/HP/273).

Happy George Washington Maeda vs. Regional Prisons Officers, Arusha, High Court of Tanzania at Arusha, Miscellaneous Criminal Cause No. 29 of 1979.

Hatimali Adamji vs. E.A.P.& T. Corporation (1973), Law Reports of Tanzania No. 6.

J. A. Garang and Others vs. the Supreme Commission of Sudan and Others, 1968, Sudan Law Reports.

Leeson vs. General Council of Medical Education and Registration, 1980, Chancery Division 366.

Lesinoi Nkeinai or Joseph Selayo Laizer and Masai Lekasi vs. Regional Prisons Officer and Regional Police Commander, High Court of Tanzania at Arusha, Miscellaneous Criminal Cause No. 22 of 1979 (unreported).

R. vs. Drybones (1970), S.C.R. 282.

R. vs. Elia Abraham and Others (1977), Resident Magistrates
    Court, Moshi (unreported).

Shaw vs. Director of Public Prosecutions (1962), A.C. 220.

Sheikh Mohamed Nassoro Abdallah vs. the Regional Police
    Commander, Dar es Salaam, High Court of Tanzania at
    Dar es Salaam, Miscellaneous Criminal Cause No. 21 of
    1983 (unreported).

Thabit Ngaka vs. Fisheries Officer (Morogoro) (1973), Law
    Reports of Tanzania, No. 24.

Underhill vs. Hernandez (1897), 168 US 250.

STATUTES

Area Commissioners Act, 1962.

Constitution (Consequential, Transitional and Temporary
    Provisions) Act, 1984 (Act Number 16 of 1984).

Deportation Ordinance (chapter 38 of the Laws of Tanzania).

Economic and Organized Crime Control Act, 1984 (Act Number
    13 of 1984).

Economic and Organized Crime Control (Amendment) Act, 1987
    (Act Number 12 of 1987).

Economic Sabotage (Special Provisions) Act, 1983 (Act
    Number 9 of 1983.

Emergency Powers Act, 1961 (Nigeria).

Emergency Powers Act, 1986 (Act Number 1 of 1986).

Employment Ordinance (Chapter 366 of the Lawls of
    Tanzania).

Expulsion of Undesirables Ordinance, 1930 (Chapter 39 of
    the Revised Laws of Tanzania).

Fifth Amendment of the State Constitution of 1984 (Act
    Number 5 of 1984).

Foreign Investments (Protection) Act, 1963 (Act Number 40
    of 1963).

Government Proceedings Act, 1967 (Act Number 16 of 1967).

Human Resources Deployment Act, 1983 (Act Number 6 of
    1983).

Insurance (Vesting of Interests and Regulations) Act, 1967
    (Act Number 4 of 1967).

Interim Constitution of Tanzania, 1965 (Chapter   596 of the
    Laws of Tanzania.

Medical Practitioners and Dentists Act, 1979 (Act Number 20
    of 1979).

Minimum Sentence Act, 1972.

National Agriculture Products Board Act, 1967 (Act Number 3
    of 1967).

National Bank of Commerce (Establishing and Vesting of
    Assets and Liabilities) Act, 1967 (Act Nuomber 1 of
    1967).

National Environment Management Act, 1983 (Act Number 19 of
    1983).

National Land Use Planning Commission Act, 1984 (Act Number
    3 of 1984).

Penal Code (chapter 16 of the Laws of Tanzania).

Permanent Commission of Enquiry Act, 1966 (Act Number 25 of
    1966).

Permanent Labour Tribunal Act, 1967 (Act Number 41 of
    1967).

Police Force Ordinance (Chapter 322 of the Revised Laws of
    Tanzania).

Political Leaders' Pensions Act, 1981.

Preservation of Public Security Act, 1966 (Act Number 18 of
    1966) (Kenya).

Presidential Elections Act, 1985 (Act Number 15 of 1985).

Professional Surveyors Act (Chapter 409 of the Laws of
    Tanzania).

Regional Commissioners Act, 1962 (Chapter 401 of the
    Revised Laws of Tanzania).

Registration and Identification of Persons Act, 1986 (Act
    Number 11 of 1986).

Resettlement of Offenders Act, 1969 (Act Number 8 of 1969).

Rural Lands (Planning and Utilization) Act, 1973 (Act
    Number 13 of 1973).

Security of Employment Act, 1962 (Chapter 574 of the Laws
    of Tanzania.

Societies Ordinance, 1954 (Chapter 337 of the Revised Laws
    of Tanzania).

Specified State Leader Retirement Benefits Act, 1986 (Act
    Number 2 of 1986).

State Trading Corporation (Establishing and Vesting of
    Interests) Act, 1967 (Act Number 2 of 1967).

Stock Theft Ordinance (Chapter 422 of the Laws of
    Tanzania).

Tanganyika Law Society Act (Chapter 334 of the Laws of
    Tanzania).

Tanganyika Preventive Detention Act, 1962 (Chapter 490 of
    the Laws of Tanzania).

Tanzania News Agency Act, 1976 (Act Number 14 of 1976).

Witchcraft Ordinance (Chapter 18 of the Laws of Tanzania).

Bibliography

Adedeji, Adebayo, and Timothy M. Shaw. Economic Crisis in
    Africa: African Perspective on Development Problems
    and Potentials. Boulder, Colo.: Lynne Rienner, 1985.

Amin, Samir, Derrick Chitala, and Ibbo Mandaza (eds.).
    SADCC Prospects for Disengagement and Development in
    Southern Africa. London: Zed Press, 1987.

Babu, A. M. African Socialism or Socialist Africa?
    London: Zed Press, 1981.

Bailey, Martin. The Union of Tanganyika and Zanzibar: A
    Study in Political Integration. Syracuse,
    N.Y.:Syracuse University Press, 1973.

Baker, M., L. Bassett, and A. Ellington. The World
    Environment Handbook: A Directory of Natural
    Resources Management and Non-Government Organizations
    in 145 Countries. New York: World Environment Center,
    1985.

Bedjaoui, Mohammed. Toward a New International Economic
    Order. New York: Holmes and Meier, 1979.

Blaustein, Albert P., and Gisbert H. Flanz (eds.).
    Constitutions of the Countries of the World, Vol.
    XVII. Dobbs Ferry, N.Y.: Oceana Publications, 1986.

Bolton, Dianne. Nationalization--A Way to Socialism? The
    Lessons of Tanzania. London: Zed Books, 1985.

Brownlie, Ian. Basic Documents on Human Rights. Oxford:
    Clarendon Press, 1981.

Buhler, Jean. Biafra: Tragödie eines begabten Volkes.
    Zurich: Schweizer Spiegel Verlag, 1968.

Carsten-Thomas, Ebenroth. Code of Conduct--Ansätze zur
    verträglichen Gestaltung Internationaler
    Investitionen. Constance: Universitätsverlag

Konstanz, 1987.

Coulson, Andrew (ed.). African Socialism in Practice: The Tanzanian Experience. Nottingham: Spokesman, 1979.

Coulson, Andrew. Tanzania: A Political Economy. Oxford: Clarendon Press, 1982.

Elian, George. The Principle of Sovereignty over Natural Resources. Alphen aan den Rijn: Sijthoff & Nordhoff, 1979.

Faundez, Julio, and Sol Picciotto (eds.). The Nationalization of Multinationals in Peripheral Economies. London: Macmillan, 1978.

Francisco, L. B., and J. S. Fast. Conspiracy for the Empire: Big Business, Corruption and the Politics of Imperialism in America, 1876-1907. Quezon City: Foundation for Nationalist Studies, 1985.

Franck, Thomas M. Human Rights in Third World Perspective, Vol. 2. New York: Oceana Publications, 1982.

Ginther, K., and W. Benedek (eds.). New Perspectives and Conceptions of International Law: An Afro-European Dialogue. Vienna: Springer-Verlag, 1983.

Godana, Bonaya Adhi. Africa's Shared Water Resources: Legal and Institutional Aspects of Nile, Niger and Senegal River Systems. London: Frances Pinter Publishers, 1985.

Gormley, W. P. Human Rights and Environment: The Need for International Cooperation. Leyden: A. W. Sijhoff, 1976.

Greenberg, Michael, and Richard F. Anderson. Hazardous Waste Sites: The Credibility Gap. New Brunswick, N.J.: Rutgers University Press, 1984.

Gstrein, Heinz. Äthiopien blickt in die Zukunft. Freiburg: Imba Verlag, 1975.

Hacker, Andrew (ed.). A Statistical Portrait of the American People. New York: Viking Press, 1983.

Hafkin, Nancy J., and Edna G. Bay (eds.). Women in Africa: Studies in Social and Economic Change. Stanford, Calif.: Stanford University Press, 1976.

Harris, Christoph, et al. Hazardous Waste: Confronting the Challenge. New York: Quorum Books, 1987.

Hayward, Fred (ed.). Elections in Independent Africa. Boulder, Colo.: Westview Press, 1987, p. 149.

Legal Aid Committee (Faculty of Law, University of Dar es Salaam). Essays on Law and Society. Kampala: Sapoba

Bookshop Press, 1985.

Legum, Colin. _Ethiopia: The Fall of Haile Selassie's Empire_. London: Rex Collings, 1975.

Lehman, John P. (ed.). _Hazardous Waste Disposal_. New York: Plenum Press, 1983.

Lenin, V. I. _Critical Remarks on the National Question: The Right of Nations to Self-Determination_. Moscow: Progress Publishers, 1971.

Lofchie, Michael F. _Zanzibar: Background to Revolution_. Princeton: Princeton University Press, 1965.

Mamdani, Mahamood. _Imperialism and Fascism in Uganda_. Nairobi: Heinemann Educational Books, 1983.

Mapolu, Henry, and Issa G. Shivji. _Vuguvugu la Wafanyakazi Nchini Tanzania_. Kampala: East Africa URM Contact Group, 1984.

Markakis, John, and Nega Ayele. _Class and Revolution in Ethiopia_. Nottingham: Spokesman, 1978.

Martin, David. _General Amin_. London: Faber and Faber, 1974.

Meagher, R. F. _An International Redistribution of Wealth and Power: A Study of the Charter of Economic Rights and Duties of States_. New York: Pergamon Press, 1979.

Mihyo, Paschal B. _Industrial Conflict and Change in Tanzania_. Dar es Salaam: Tanzania Publishing House.

Mittelman, James H. _Underdevelopment and Transition to Socialism: Mozambique and Tanzania_. New York: Academic Press, 1981.

Morrision, David R. _Education and Politics in Africa: The Tanzania Case_. London: C. Hurst and Company, 1976.

Nabudere, D. W. _Essays on the Theory and Practice of Imperialism_. London: Onyx Press, 1979.

Nordquist, Myron H. (ed.). _United Nations Convention on the Law of the Sea: A Commentary_, Vol. 1, Dordrecht: Martinus Nijhoff Publishers, 1985.

Nsekela, A. J. (ed.). _Southern Africa: Toward Economic Liberation_. London: Rex Collings, 1981.

Nyerere, J. K. _Freedom and Development_. Dar es Salaam: Oxford University Press, 1967.

_____. _Freedom and Unity_. Dar es Salaam: Oxford University Press, 1967.

_____. Freedom and Socialism. Dar es Salaam: Oxford University Press, 1968.

_____. Bildung und Befreiung. Frankfurt: Verlag Otto Lembeck, 1977.

O'Ballance, Edgar. The Secret War in the Sudan. London: Faber & Faber, 1977.

O'Connel, D. P. International Law, 2nd Ed. Vol. 1. London: Stevens and Sons, 1970.

Oduho, Joseph, and William Deng. The Problem of the Southern Sudan. London: Oxford University Press, 1963.

Oellers-Frahm, Karin, and Norbert Wuhler (eds.). Dispute Settlement in Public International Law: Texts and Materials. Berlin: Springer Verlag, 1984.

Poppe, Eberhard (ed.). Grundrechte des Burgers in der Sozialistischen Gesellschaft. Berlin: Staatsverlag der Deutschen Demokratischen Republik, 1980.

Potyka, Christian. Haile Selassie: Der Negus Negesti in Frieden und Krieg. Bad Honnef: Osang Verlag, 1974.

Pratt, Cranford. The Critical Phase in Tanzania, 1945-1968: Nyerere and the Emergence of a Socialist Strategy. Cambridge: Cambridge University Press, 1976.

Renger, Annemarie. Gleiche Chancen für Frauen? Heidelberg: C. F. Muller Juristischer Verlag, 1977.

Resnick, Idrian N . The Long Transition: Building of Socialism in Tanzania. New York: Monthly Review Press, 1981.

Rigo-Sureda, A. The Evolution of the Right to Self-Determination. Leiden: A. W. Sijhoff, 1973.

Rimmer, Douglas. The Economies of West Africa. New York: St. Martin's Press, 1984.

Robertson, Claire C. (ed.). Women and Slavery in Africa. Madison: University of Wisconsin Press, 1984.

Robson, Peter. Integration, Development and Equity: Economic Integration in West Africa. London: Allen & Unwin, 1983.

Schindler, Dietrich, and Jiri Toman (eds.). The Law of Armed Conflicts: A Collection of Conventions, Resolutions and Other Documents. Alphen aan den Rijn: Sijthoff & Noordhoff, 1981.

Schwazenberger, Georg. International Law, Vol. 1. London: Stevens and Sons, 1976.

Seeburg, Gustav.   Die Wahrheit über Nigerias Biafra:
    Vorgeschichte und Hintergrunde des Konfliktes. Bern:
    Verlag Paul Haupt, 1969.

Sesay, Amadu, et al.   The OAU after Twenty Years. Boulder,
    Colo. Westview Press, 1984.

Shivji, Issa G.   Silent Class Struggle.   Dar es Salaam:
    Tanzania Publishing House, 1973.

_____.   Class Struggles in Tanzania. London: Heinemann,
    1976.

_____.   Law, State and the Working Class in Tanzania.
    London: James Currey, 1986.

Shukri, M. A.   The Concept of Self-Determination in the
    United Nations. Damascus: Al Jadidah Press, 1965.

Sinare, Hawa. Legal and Economic Effects of Expropriation
    and Nationalization of Foreign Investments.
    Constance: Wolfgang Haltung-Gorre Verlag, 1983.

Sornarajah, M.   The Pursuit of Nationalized Property.
    Dordrecht: Martinus Nijhoff, 1986.

Spretnak, C.   Die Grünen: Nicht links nicht rechts sondern
    vorne. Munich: Wilhelm Goldmann Verlag, 1985.

Starushenko, G.   The Principle of National Self-Deter-
    mination in Soviet Foreign Policy. Moscow: Foreign
    Languages Publishing House, 1963.

Stremlau, John J.   The International Politics of the
    Nigerian Civil War, 1967-1970. Princeton: Princeton
    University Press, 1977.

Thiong'O, Ngugi Wa.   Detained: A Writer's Prison Diary.
    London: Heinemann, 1981.

Umozurike, U. O.   Self-Determination in International Law.
    Hamden, Conn.: Archon Books, 1972.

United Nations.   Yearbook on Human Rights for 1977-1978.
    New York: UN Secretariat, 1982.

Ustorf, Werner. Afrikanische Initiative: Des aktive Leiden
    des Propheten Simon Kimbangu.   Bern: Herbert Lang,
    1975.

Vasak, Karel (ed.).   The International Dimensions of Human
    Rights, Vol. 2.   Westport, Conn.: Greenwood Press,
    1982.

Von Freyhold, M. Ujamaa Villages in Tanzania: Analysis of
    a Social Experiment.   London: Heinemann Educational
    Books, 1979.

Weeks, Kent M. _Ombudsmen around the World: A Comparative Chart_. Berkeley: Institute of Governmental Studies, 1978.

Welch, Claude E., Jr. and Ronald I. Meltzer (eds.). _Human Rights and Development in Africa_. Albany: State University of New York Press, 1984.

Whyte, John D. and William R. Ledermann. _Canadian Constitutional Law_. Toronto: Butterworths, 1977.

Winzeler, Christoph. _Die politischen Rechte des Aktivburgers nach schweizerischem Bundesrecht_. Basel: Helbing & Lichtenhan, 1983.

Wolf, Erik. _Ordnung der Kirche: Lehr- und Handbuch des Kirchenrechts aus Ökumenischer Basis_. Frankfurt: Vittorio Kostermann, 1961.

Wolfers, Michael. _Politics in the Organization of African Unity_. London: Methuen & Co., 1976.

World Commission on Environment and Development. _Our Common Future_. Oxford: Oxford University Press, 1988.

Wubneh, Mulatu, and Yohanis Abate. _Ethiopia: Transition and Development in the Horn of Africa_. Boulder, Colo.: Westview Press, 1988.

Yardley, D. C. M. _Principles of Administrative Law_. London: Butterworths, 1981.

Yeager, Rodger. _Tanzania: An African Experiment_. Boulder, Colo.: Westview Press, 1982.

Zacklin, R., and L. Caflisch (eds.). _The Legal Regime of International Rivers and Lakes_. The Hague: Martinus Nijhoff, 1981.

Zulch, Tilman, and Klaus, Guercke (eds.). _Soll Biafra überleben? Dokumente-Berichte-Analysen-Kommentare_. Berlin: Lettner Verlag, 1969.

ARTICLES

Abrahams, Ray. "Sungu Sungu: Village Vigilante Groups in Tanzania. Volume 86, No. 343, _African Affairs_, 1987, p. 179.

Akinyemi, A., Bolaji. "The Organization of African Unity and the Concept of Non-Interference in the Internal Affairs of Member-States." Volume 46, _British Yearbook of International Law_, 1972-73, p. 393.

Alson, P. "Develoopment and the Rule of Law: Prevention versus Cure as a Human Rights Strategy." In International Commission of Jurists, _Development,_

Human Rights and Rule of Law. Oxford: Pergamon Press, 1981, p. 31.

Anglin, Douglas G. "SADCC after Nkomati." Volume 84, No. 335, _African Affairs_, 1984, p. 163.

Asante, Samuel K. B. "National Building and Human Rights in Emergent African Nations." Volume 2, _Cornell International Law Journal_, 1969, p. 72.

Ayittey, George. "African Freedom of Speech." Volume 16, No. 1, _Index on Censorship_, January 1987, p. 16.

Baxi, Upendra. "The New International Economic Order, Basic Needs and Rights: Notes Towards Development of the Right to Development." Volume 23, _Indian Journal of International Law_, 1983, p. 225.

Bedjaoui, Mohammed. "Right to Development and Jus Cogens." In Milan Bulajic, Dimitrije Pindic, and Momirka Marinkovic, _The Charter of Economic Rights and Duties of States: Ten Years of Implementation_. Belgrade: Institute of International Politics and Economy, 1986, p. 43.

Blay, S. Kwaw Nyameke. "Changing African Perspectives on the Right to Self-Determination in the Wake of the Banjul Charter on Human and People's Rights." Volume 29, _Journal of African Studies_, 1985, p. 147.

Bradley, A. W. "The Nationalizations of Companies in Tanzania." In P. A. Thomas, _Private Enterprise and the East African Company_, Dar es Salaam: Tanzania Publishing House, 1969.

Casin, Rene. "Introduction: The International Law of Human Rights." Volume 144, _Receuls des Cours_, 1974.

D'sa, Rose M. "Human and People's Rights: Distinctive Features of the African Charter." Volume 29, _Journal of African Studies_, 1985, p. 72.

De Kadt, Emmanuel. "Some Basic Questions on Human Rights and Development." Volume 8, _World Development_, 1980, p. 97.

Dias, Clarence. "Tanzanian Nationalizations: 1967-70." Volume 4, No. 1, _Cornell International Law Journal_, 1970, p. 59.

Dickstein, H . L. "International Lake and River Pollution Control: Questions of Methods." Volume 12, _Columbia Journal of Transnational Law_, 1973.

Donnolly, Jack. "The 'Right to Development'; How Not to Link Human Rights and Development." In C. E. Welch, Jr., and R. I. Meltzer, _Human Rights and Development in Africa_. Albany: State University of New York Press, 1984, Chapter 12.

_____. "Human Rights and Development: Complementary or Competing Concerns?" In G. W. Shepherd, Jr., and V. P. Nanda, Human Rights and Third World Development, Westport, Conn.: Greenwood Press, 1985, p. 48.

Dunnebier, Anna.   "Mustrprozess: Gleicher Lohn für gleiche Arbeit." Emma, August 1978, p. 48.
Eagleton, Clyde.   "Self-Determination and the United Nations."   Volume 47, American Journal of International Law, 1953, p. 88.

Fahmi, Aziza M. "The Degree of Effectiveness of International Law as Regards International Rivers." Volume 28, Österreichische Zeitschrift für öfftentliches Recht und Völkerrect, 1977.

Fatouros, A. A.   "The UN Code of Conduct of Transnational Corporations: Problems of   Interpretation and Implementation."   In Seymour J. Rubin and Gary Clyde Hufbauer, Emerging Standards of International Trade and Investment.   New York: West Publishing Company, 1985, p. 101.

Francioni, Francesco. "Compensation for Nationalization of Foreign Property: The Borderline between Law and Equity." Volume 24, International and Comparative Law Quarterly, 1975.

Fuller, Lon L. "Positivism and Fidelity to Law--A Reply to Professor Hart." Volume 71, No. 4, Harvard Law Review, 1958, p. 630.

Ghai, Yash.   "Law and Public Enterprise in Tanzania." In Law in the Political Economy of Public Enterprise. Uppsala: Scandinavian Institute of African Studies, 1977.

Gordon, David F. "Foreign Relations: Dilemmas of Independence and Development."   In Joel D. Barkan, Politics and Public Policy in Kenya and Tanzania, Rev. Ed. New York: Praeger, 1984.

Green, Reginald H. "A Guide to Acquisition and Initial Operation: Reflections from Tanzanian Experience, 1967-1974." In Julio Faundez and Sol Picciotto, The Nationalization of Multinationals in Peripheral Economies. London: Macmillan, 1978.

Hardy, Michael.   "The United Nations Environment Program." In Ludwik A. Teclaff and Albert E. Utton, International Environmental Law. New York: Praeger, 1974, p. 57.

Hart, H. L. A. "Positivism and the Separation of Law and Morals." Volume 71, No. 4, Harvard Law Review, 1958, p. 593.

House, William J. "The Status of Women in the Sudan." Volume 26, No. 2, Journal of Modern African Studies, pp. 277-302.

Kalunga, L. T. "Human Rights and the Preventive Detention Act, 1962 of the United Republic of Tanzania: Some Operative Aspects." Volumes 11-14, Eastern African Law Review, 1978-81, p. 281.

Kannyo, Edward.   "The Banjul Charter on Human and People's Rights: Genesis and Political Background." In Claude E. Welch, Jr., and Ronald I. Meltzer, Human Rights and Development in Africa. Albany: State University of New York Press, 1984, p. 128.

Kiss, Alexandre.   "The International Protection of the Environment." In R. St. J. MacDonald and Johnston D. M. Douglas, The Structure and Process of International Law: Essays in Legal Philosophy, Doctrine and Theory. The Hague: Martinus Nijhoff, 1983, p. 1069.

Kiwanuka, Richard N.   "The Meaning of 'People' in the African Charter on Human and People's Rights." Volume 80, American Journal of International Law, 1988, p. 80.

Kumar, Umesh.   "African Response to the International Economic Order: Lagos Plan of Action and Preferential Trade Area Treaty for the Eastern and Southern African States." Volume 5, Jahrbuch für afrikan- isches Recht/Yearbook for African Law, 1984, p. 81.

Kunig, Philip. "The Protection of Human Rights by Interna- tional Law in Africa." Volume 25, German Yearbook of International Law, 1982, p. 138.

Levin, D. B. "Self-Determination of Nations in interna- tional Law." Soviet Yearbook of International Law, 1962, p. 46.

MacDermot, Niall. "The Ombudsman Institution." The Review of International Commission of Jurists, No. 21, December 1978, p. 37.

Malima, Kighoma A. "IMF and World Bank Conditionality: The Tanzanian Case." In Peter Lawrence, World Recession and the Food Crisis in Africa. London: James Currey, 1986, pp. 129-39.

M'baye, Keba.   "Le droit au developpment comme un droit de l'homme." Volume 5, Nos. 2-3, Revue des droits de l'homme/Human Rights Journal, 1972.

_____. "We Have to Fight More and More for the Right to Development." No. 111, The Courier, September- October, 1988, p. 2.

McAuslan, J. P. W. B., and Yash P. Ghai. "Constitutional Innovation and Political Stability in Tanzania: A Preliminary Assessment." Volume 4, No. 4, Journal of Modern African Studies, 1966, p. 479.

Meisler, Stanley. "Holocaust in Burundi, 1972." In Willem
    A. Veenhoven, Case Studies on Human Rights and
    Fundamental Freedoms: A World Survey.   The Hague:
    Martinus Nijhoff, 1976, p. 225.

Meynes, Peter. "Southern African Development Co-ordination
    Conference (SADCC) and Regional Co-Operation in
    Southern Africa."   In   Domenico Mazzeo, African
    Regional   Organizations.   .   Cambridge: Cambridge
    University Press, 1984.

Mihyo, Paschal.   "The Struggle for Workers' Control in
    Tanzania." Review of African Political Economy, May-
    October 1975, p. 62.

Mlimuka, A. K. L. J., and P. J. A. M. Kabudi. " The State
    and the Party." In Issa G. Shivji, The State and the
    Working People in Tanzania. Dakar: CODESRIA, 1986.

Mullings, Leith.   "Women and Economic Change in Africa."
    In Nancy J. Hafkin and Edna G. Bay, Women in Africa:
    Studies in Social and Economic Change. Stanford,
    Calif.: Stanford University Press, 1976, p. 239.

Mwasem, Ngila.   "The African Preferential Trade Area:
    Towards a Sub-Regional Economic Community in Eastern
    and Southern Africa." Volume 19, Journal of World
    Trade Law, 1985, p. 622

Neerso, Peter.   "Tanzania's Policies on Private Foreign
    Investment." Volume 19, Journal of World Trade Law,
    1985, p. 622.

Norton, Patrick M. "The Tanzanian Ombudsman." Volume 22,
    The International and Comparative Law Quarterly, 1973,
    p. 603.

Okidi, C. O. "Legal and Policy Regime of Lake Victoria and
    Nile Basins."   Volume 20,   Indian Journal of
    International Law, 1980.

Olanrewaji, S. A., and Toyin Falola. "Development through
    Integration: The Politics and Problems of ECOWAS." In
    Olusola Akinrinade and J. Kurt Barling, Economic
    Development in Africa: International Efforts, Issues
    and Prospects. London: Pinter Publishers, 1987.

Oluyede, Peter.   "Redress of Grievances in Tanzania."
    Public Law, 1975, p. 8.

Omwony Ojwok. "Who is to Lead the Popular Anti-Imperialist
    Revolution in Africa: In Refutation of Issa G.
    Shivji's Petty-Bourgeoios Neo-Marxist Line." In Yash
    Tandon, Debate on Class, State and Imperialism. Dar
    es Salaam: Tanzania Publishing House, 1982.

Owosekun, A. "Some Thorny Issues in the Economic Community
    of West Africa."   In W. A. Ndongo, Economic Co-
    operation and Integration in Africa. Dakar: CODESRIA,

1985.

Palmeira, S.   "The Principle of Self-Determination in
    International Law."   No. 1(3), International
    Association of Democratic Lawyers Review, 1954.

Peter, C. M. "Report: Tanzania Marine Policy." Volume 7,
    No. 1, Marine Policy: The International Journal of
    Ocean Affairs, 1983, pp. 58-59.

_____.   "Mercenaries and International Humanitarian
    Law."   Volume 24, No. 3, Indian Journal of
    International Law, 1984, p. 373.

_____.   "Justice in a One-Party African State: The
    Tanzanian Experience--A Rejoinder." Volume 20, No. 2,
    Verfassung und Recht in Übersee, 1987, p. 235.

Peter, Chris, and Sengondo Mvungi. "The State and Student
    Struggles." In Issa G. Shivji, The State and the
    Working People in Tanzania. Dakar: CODESRIA, 1986.

Quigley, John.   "Cases on Preventive Detention: A Review."
    Volumes 11-14, Eastern African Law Review, 1978-81, p.
    326.

Rabl, Kurt. "Constitutional Development and the Law of the
    United Republic of Tanzania: An Outline."   Volume 16,
    Jahrbuch des öffentlichen Rechts der Gegenwart, 1967,
    p. 567.

Rauch, Elmar.   "The Compatibility of the Detention of
    Terrorists Order (Northern Ireland) with European
    Convention for the Protection of Human Rights."
    Volume 6, No. 1, New York University Journal of
    International Law and Politics, 1973, p. 1.

Ravenhill, John.   "Collective Self-Reliance or Collective
    Self-Delusion: Is the Lagos Plan a Viable
    Alternative?" In Africa in Economic Crisis. London:
    Macmillan, 1986.

Read, J. S. "Bills of Rights in the Third World, Some
    Commonwealth Experiences."   Volume 6, Verfassung und
    Recht in Übersee, 1973, p. 21.

Ringera, A. G. "The African Charter on Human and People's
    Rights: A Comment." Volume 3, The Advocate (Nairobi),
    1984, p. 15.

Rwelamira, M. R. K.   "Contemporary Self-Determination and
    the United Nations Charter: An Appraisal of the Use
    of Force against Colonialism and Racial Discrimination
    in Southern Africa." Volume 6, No. 3, African Review,
    1976.

Sand, P. H. "Development of International Law in the Lake
    Chad Development Basin." Volume 34, Zeitschrift für
    ausländisches Recht und Völkerrecht, 1974.

Sesay, Amadu.   "The Role of the Frontline States in Southern Africa." In Olajide Aluko and Timothy M. Shaw, <u>Southern Africa in the 1980s</u>. London: Allen and Unwin, 1983.

Shivji, Issa G.   "The State of the Constitution and the Constitution of the State in Tanzania." Volumes 11-14, <u>Eastern African Law Review</u>, 1978-81, p. 1.

Sinare, Hawa. "The Implication of the Preferential Trade Area for Economic Integration in Eastern and Southern Africa." In Ibrahim S. R. Msabaha and Timothy M. Shaw, <u>Confrontation and Liberation in Southern Africa: Regional Directions after the Nkomati Accord</u>. Boulder, Colo.: Westview Press, 1987.

Strobel, Margaret.   "From Lelemama to Lobbying: Women's Associations in Mombasa, Kenya."   In Nancy J. Hafkin and Edna G. Bay, <u>Women in Africa: Studies in Social and Economic Change</u>.   Stanford, Calif.: Stanford University Press, 1976, p. 183.

Strong, F.   "A Global Imperative." In T. C. Emmel, <u>Global Perspective for Ecology</u>. Palo Alto, Calif.: Mayfield Publishing Company, 1977, Chapter 33.

Symonides, J . "International Legal Problems of the Fight Against Pollution of the Rivers." Volume 5, <u>Polish Yearbook of International Law</u>, 1972-73.

Szabo, Imre.   "Fundamental Questions Concerning the Theory of History of Citizens' Rights." In Jozsef Halasz, <u>Socialist Concept of Human Rights</u>. Budapest: Akademiai Kiado, 1966, pp. 27-81.

Umozurika, UY. O.   "The African Charter on Human and People's Rights."   Volume 77, <u>American Journal of International Law</u>, 1983, p. 902.

Vasak, Karel. "Human Rights: A   Thirty-Year Struggle." <u>UNESCO Courier</u>, November 1977.

Weeramantry, C. G. "The Right to Development." Volume 25, <u>Indian Journal of International Law</u>, 1985, p. 482.

Welch, Claude E., Jr.   "The OAU and Human Rights: Towards a New Definition."   Volume 19, No. 3, <u>Journal of Modern African Studies</u>, 1981, p. 401.

Williams, David V. "Law and Socialist Rural Development." Volume 6, No. 3. <u>Eastern Africa Law Review</u>, 1973, p. 193.

Zander, Michael. "The Act of State Doctrine."   Volume 53, <u>American Journal of International Law</u>, 1959, p. 826.

Index